2nd Edition

Internships, Volume 2: Newspaper, Magazine and Book Publishing

2nd Edition

Internships, Volume 2: Newspaper, Magazine and Book Publishing

Series Editor: Ronald W. Fry

The Career Press
62 Beverly Rd.
PO Box 34
Hawthorne, NJ 07507
1-800-CAREER-1
FAX: 201-427-2037

Articles by Donald McAllister, Jr., Bill Winkelman and Robert E. Kenyon, Jr. were adapted from articles that appeared in our *Magazines Career Directory* (4th edition); articles by Nat Bodian and Les Petriw were adapted from articles appearing in our *Book Publishing Career Directory* (4th edition); articles by Valerie Salembier, Anthony Geiorgianni and Mary Kay Blake were adapted from those appearning in our *Newspapers Career Directory* (3rd edition). All of these volumes are copyright 1990 The Career Press Inc.

The Internship Series

Internships, Volume 2: Newspaper, Magazine and Book Publishing, 2nd Edition, ISBN 0-934829-66-7, $11.95

Copies of this volume may be ordered by mail or phone directly from the publisher. To order by mail, please include price as noted above, $2.50 handling per order, plus $1.00 for each book ordered. Send to: The Career Press Inc., 62 Beverly Rd., PO Box 34, Hawthorne, NJ 07507

Or call Toll-Free 1-800-CAREER-1 (in Canada: 201-427-0229) to order using your VISA or Mastercard or for further information on all books published or distributed by The Career Press.

Table of Contents

Section 4: Appendices & Indexes

Foreword

Organizing Your Internship Search

If you're sure you want a career in some area of publishing—whether the daily excitement of fast-breaking news, the challenge of surpassing last's month's magazine issue or dealing with today's literary lions at the (seemingly) more leisurely pace of a book publishing house—there are courses to take, reams of information to study, techniques to master. But perhaps most important of all, there are **internships.**

Just what *is* an internship? Part audition, part test, part question, part answer. Lasting for a summer or, during the school-year, for a semester, interns are usually college students "trying out" their career by working in a professional (or near-professional) capacity at a newspaper, magazine or book publishing house. For a limited time, without the Damoclean fear of "choosing the wrong career," you actually are able to learn first-hand about the industry, company and even the specific job function you expect to head for after graduation. To turn your reading into real day-to-day experience... and find out all the things no book can hope to tell you anyway. Best of all, many of these publishers will actually pay you to "test drive" your future career!

It's not all largess—internships are a double-edged sword, good for you and the company that hires you. While you get the chance to test drive a reporter's beat, learn how to sell ad space for a major consumer magazine or publicize a book house's latest best-seller candidate, the publishers get the chance to take a look at you...and all the other students out there who are, after all, the "new blood" entering the industry.

Not surprisingly, many of these publishers make a point of hiring interns back after graduation or, at the very least, giving them precedence over other candidates for scarce entry-level jobs. Why not? They've had upwards of three months to test drive *you*, a period which has certainly told them whether or not they want you around for *more* than just a summer.

What If You Aren't Sure About Publishing?

While this volume features articles by top professionals in each industry on how to specifically go about getting an internship in their field, we *are* assuming you already know something about the field and have decided to pursue a publishing internship. It is *not* meant to convince you that one of these areas of publishing is the right one for you.

If you aren't sure and want to get a better "feel" for the many specializations within each publishing industry, the three books we most strongly recommend are our *Newspapers Career Directory, Magazines Career Directory* and *Book Publishing Career Directory*. Together, they feature some six dozen articles by top professionals in each field covering every specialty. With detailed information about current salaries, career paths, recommended courses and majors and what you'll be doing as an entry-level person in each department, these articles will surely help you gain a broader understanding of each industry and provide the detailed information you need to decide exactly what you want to do.

In addition to these acclaimed volumes, ask your local librarian for other books on these fields written by the people who've worked in them. There are many of them. Such "I was there" books will give you more of the first-hand information you need to know to decide whether any of these industries is really right for you.

And talk to your journalism professors. Many of them have extensive experience in publishing and can tell you what is good and bad about each area.

Using This Internships Volume

Assuming you have, at least for now, decided to pursue a career in one of the three areas of publishing and are seeking an internship to "test the waters," this volume is definitely the single book you need.

Its three sections cover each of the three areas of publishing: newspaper, magazine and book. While all are involved with "publishing" *something*, they are really different industries...different enough that transferring from one to another is difficult. While you *will* need to decide which area to enter after graduation, you do not have to be quite as decisive while seeking an internship. Presuming you are otherwise qualified for a specific job, a newspaper will not penalize you for spending last summer on a magazine internship.

In each section, we have included an article on the field in general, one or two specific articles on how to get an internship in that field or what an entry-level job in that field is like, and detailed listings of those publishers offering internships. These listings, gathered through our own telephone surveys, offer more information on more publishers than any book ever published, everything from the specific contact to the application deadline. By utilizing this previously-unavailable information, you will be well on your way to landing the position you want.

And note that this new second edition now includes articles on breaking into the fields in Canada and listings of top Canadian publishers.

Other References To Consult

Despite this overabundance of information, you may not have everything you need. Seeking an internship is very much like seeking a job—anything you know about the company or person you're trying to work for can only help. So as you begin your search and, especially, begin to narrow it down to the chosen few, you may want to consult other reference resources, both those specific to the publishing industry and those covering all industries.

If you're interested in book publishing, consider <u>Literary Marketplace</u> (<u>LMP</u>)—available from R. R. Bowker (245 West 17th St., New York, NY 10011)—the natural companion to this volume. It lists all of the houses we've featured in chapter 12 (plus hundreds more) and offers a plethora of additional listings of companies and services allied with the book business. If you're seeking an overseas internship, another Bowker publication—<u>International Literary Marketplace</u>—is an invaluable source. It lists more than 9,000 publishers in 160 countries. Check you library—it costs nearly $100.00.

R. R. Bowker also publishes two excellent reference works for the magazine industry—<u>Magazine Industry Marketplace</u> and <u>Ulrich's International Periodicals Directory.</u> The former details most of the major magazines published in the U.S.; the latter nearly every one published throughout the world (though with substantially less information on each title and even less on the companies that publish them). A similar volume, the <u>Standard Periodical Directory,</u> is available from Oxbridge Communications (183 Madison Ave., Suite 1108, New York, NY 10016). All three of these reference works should be available at your local or school library.

A key reference resource on newspapers is the Editor & Publisher International Yearbook, an annual publication that lists U.S. and Canadian dailies and weeklies, foreign newspapers, news services, major newspaper groups and pertinent organizations (city state and regional press associations, schools and departments of journalism, etc.). It should be available in virtually any public or school library.

Less complete information on most U.S. papers is included in the various editions of Standard Rate and Data Service (SRDS), the bible of ad agency media buyers. Much of the information, however, isn't directly pertinent to *your* areas of concern—you'll find, for example, virtually no information on the publishing *companies*.

For more general research (pertinent to all publishers), you might want to start with How To Find Information About Companies (Washington Researchers, 1985); the Encyclopedia of Business Information Sources (Gale Research, Book Tower, Detroit, MI 48226); and/or the Guide to American Directories (B. Klein Publications, P.O. Box 8503, Coral Springs, FL 33065), which lists directories for over 3,000 fields.

If you want to intern at one of the associations which serves the publishing industry (or the fields with which it's most closely allied), we've listed all those in chapter 13. Other associations may be researched in the Encyclopedia of Associations (Gale Research Co.) or National Trade and Professional Associations of the United States (Columbia Books, Inc., 777 14th St., NW, Suite 236, Washington, DC 20005).

There are, in addition, many general corporate directories, biographical indexes, statistical abstracts, etc., etc.—from Gale Research, Dun & Bradstreet, Standard & Poor's, Ward's and others—which may give you additional information on major publishers and their executives. These volumes should all be available in the reference (and/or business) section of your local library.

Organizing Your Approach

What to do before you start your research:

• Collect all necessary records to prepare your resume; write and print sufficient quantities.

• Collect and organize your writing samples, published clips, art or photographic portfolio.

• Prepare basic formats for the cover letters you will be required to write.

• Decide the basic parameters of your search—i.e., specific kind of publishers (large daily newspapers only, consumer magazines, etc.), geographical areas you would consider, whether salary is important (or necessary), etc. Put these criteria on a single sheet so you can make sure the publishers you target satisfy all of them.

• Make sure you start early enough and allow enough time for all the record-collecting, resume-preparing, letter-writing and information-gathering chores a successful internship search will require.

Hints on utilizing the research information you collect:

• Start the submission process as early as possible; whatever the printed deadline, attempt to have all your applications, resumes, etc. on publishers' desks long before. This is a very competitive arena—you can't lose by being first on the scene.

• Attempt to narrow your search as soon as possible so you can supply the information required in a timely fashion.

• Make sure you follow instructions verbatim. If writing samples are required, for example, don't fail to include them in your application package.

• If a separate application form is required, write (or call) to obtain it as early as available so you have enough time to fill it out completely. Some require mini-biographies, detailed answers to complicated questions, etc. Take the time to make each application as complete and professional as possible.

• As you begin your search, establish a system to keep track of each step with each publisher. Utilize either a separate file folder or a note card system so you always know what's due when, what's completed, what's still to do, when you can expect to hear from each, etc. The more organized your records, the more likely you won't miss a deadline or fail to complete a required submission.

If You Need More Help

It is beyond the scope of this book to help you organize your resume, learn the correct way to write cover letters, organize your portfolio or lead you through the interview process (and some companies do require in-person interviews).

If you need help with resumes or cover letters, there are a number of excellent resume books in your local library. The two we recommend are Your First Resume (2nd Edition) by Ronald W. Fry, the first book written expressly for high school and college students only, and the brand-new College Student's Resume Guide by Kim Marino (both are available through The Career Press).

For interviewing, the 1990 edition of Interview for Success by Dr. Ron Krannich (also available through The Career Press) is the best we've seen.

In any event, good luck in your search. Your internship will give you the first real taste of the world of publishing, a fascinating, exciting, rewarding world, indeed!

Section 1

Internships In Newspaper Publishing

1

Newspaper Work: A Classic American Occupation

Valerie B. Salembier, President
New York Post

Newspapers reflect the cultures in which they exist. They come in all shapes and sizes, differ in reporting methods and editorial views, and sell for different prices. Newspapers are how the overwhelming portion of the world's literate population learns about local, national, and international events.

As Americans, newspaper ink is in our blood. Freedom of the Press is an American concept. Imagine that, we *invented* the concept of a free press!

We respect that freedom. Americans don't respond to slanderous or slanted reporting. We want investigative reporting. We want to know everything about our elected officials. In fact, we generally want to know everything—or at least have the option to know.

Newspapers allow us those options in a detailed and personal way that other mediums cannot. As long as our national mystique demands an open and open-minded society, newspapers will continue to thrive.

The Legacy Of A Free Press

Alexander Hamilton founded the *New York Post* in 1801. That makes us the oldest continuously-published daily newspaper in the United States. We take that honor seriously. We strive to serve our readers daily. And that takes hard work from a multitude of different people in a complex (and often confusing) mosaic of jobs.

Those of you thinking about a career in newspapers will hear from many that ink and paper are an anachronism soon to disappear. Not so. Progress does not mean abandonment. American newspapers, a unique extension of our national character, are here to stay.

If you're thinking about a newspaper career, I strongly recommend that you pursue it. The rewards are enormous.

Newspapers As Business

Newspapers are a business, and are in business to make a profit. There are two sides to this aspect of newspapering.

Circulation is the bread and butter of the business side of every newspaper. The more people who buy copies of a paper every day, the more revenue comes back to the home office. Circulation is a science. Not just *where* you distribute, but *how* and *when* and *how many*.

Circulation is often best known for games and contests devised to build readership. As *Reader's Digest* (with a circulation of over 16,250,000) offers sweepstakes worth millions of dollars to attract subscribers, so newspapers create sweepstakes to generate excitement and boost sales. This may sound like fun (and it is), but it's not easy.

It's not enough to ask what type of contest or consumer promotion will attract the *most* readers. Circulation must devise games and other promotions that attract the right *kind* of reader—one who is a good match for the editorial style of the newspaper, and equally important, will continue buying the paper long after the contest has run its course. Not a simple task. Many try, few succeed.

Advertising Sales is the second leg of the newspaper business. In many ways, it is both the most satisfying and the most difficult.

When you read a newspaper you see ads for stores, movies, banks, etc. Those advertisers pay to have their product message appear within the pages of a newspaper. It is the job of advertising sales representatives to convince a potential advertiser that their newspaper is the correct environment for a particular sales message.

The ad salesperson must be able to use research (such as readership, age/income demographics, and product usage information), along with promotional materials (brochures, premiums, and merchandising opportunities) to prove why that particular newspaper is a wise and efficient "buy."

I'm sure you've all heard about the famous two-hour lunches ad salespeople enjoy. Well, let me assure you all that lunch with a client is twice as hard as an office meeting. Selling space is a tough, competitive undertaking. It takes intelligence, personality skills, and tenacity. It's never easy to get someone to spend their ad dollars. And that's truer in newspapers than anyplace else.

Newspapers As Product

Business is business. And the only way for Circulation to sell papers and for Advertising Sales to do its job is to have a solid product—a terrific newspaper.

There's nothing gimmicky about a good newspaper. Technology has changed newspapers as it has changed almost every other facet of modern life. The cacophony of clicking city room typewriters has been replaced by the more advanced clicking of word processors—but the job remains the same.

A newspaper has to be accurate, timely, biting, entertaining, authoritative, thought provoking, comforting, feisty, fun, and *necessary*.

At the *New York Post,* we publish a daily road map to help our readers walk through the system. H.L. Mencken wrote that "Newspapers should comfort the afflicted and afflict the comfortable." That's still the best definition I've come across of what a good newspaper should be.

That job starts with the editor and continues with every member of the editorial staff—from seasoned pro to cub reporter. What they all share is a sense of mission. They all share the enthusiasm to produce the best articles every day. That's the beauty of a newspaper—there's a new product daily.

How To Get That First Job

One of the most common questions I'm asked is, "How can I get a job at a newspaper?" My response is always the same, and it's based on something that happened at one of our daily 4 pm editorial meetings (where we decide what's going in the next day's paper).

Jerry Nachman, our editor, asked a reporter if he had gotten a photograph of an underworld bigwig and his flamboyant chauffeur/bodyguard. The reporter responded that since it didn't seem likely to happen, he hadn't asked. Nachman's measured reply, "You don't ask, you don't get."

So, if you think there's some special magic to getting a job at the *Post* or any other newspaper, think again. All it takes is talent, drive, aggressiveness, high energy and a real desire to work for one of our greatest American institutions—the Free Press.

That's true for every aspect of the newspaper business, from production to circulation, ad sales, editorial, and the many other jobs that it takes to turn out a newspaper. Each of these areas is discussed at length in the *Newspapers Career Directory,* for which this article was orginially written. I strongly suggest you get a copy of this book and read all its articles. A broad base of knowledge is, as always, the shortest route to success.

I'm sure that Alexander Hamilton is smiling.

Named president of the *Post* in April, 1989, **VALERIE B. SALEMBIER** is responsible for the newspaper's business, advertising sales, and circulation operations.

Prior to joining the *Post,* Ms. Salembier, 44, was publisher of *TV Guide,* the nation's largest circulation periodical. Previously, she was senior vice president, advertising of *USA Today.* Her five-year tenure at the nation's first national daily saw revenues increase from $38 million to $140 million.

Ms. Salembier has also served as vice president and publisher of 13/30 Corporation's Student Publication Division (now part of Whittle Communications), publisher of *Inside Sports* magazine, and advertising sales director and associate publisher of *Ms.* magazine.

In 1972, Ms. Salembier became the first woman to serve on the advertising sales staff of *Newsweek* magazine. She began her publishing career in promotion at Time, Inc.

An avid sports fan, Ms. Salembier is one of the authors of the original Rotisserie League Baseball, published by Bantam Books in 1984. She is a resident of Manhattan and a graduate of the College of New Rochelle.

2

Your Life As A Young Reporter

Anthony Giorgianni, Reporter
The Hartford Courant

Imagine having the opportunity to explore things you have always wondered about, but never really had the time to investigate or experience: Spending the day at an air show, asking the pilots what it's like to travel in a high-speed, tight formation. Visiting a courtroom, watching attorneys argue complex legal issues that will determine the fate of someone accused of a serious crime. Or going to supermarkets and buying dozens of items, just to confirm your suspicion that consumers are being charged more than they should be.

That is how news reporters spend most of their day: learning. The rest of their time is spent trying to interpret what they have learned and deciding the best way to present that information to the public.

The reporter's world is certainly one for people who like to take things apart, examine how they work, then put them back together. We are given many opportunities to do just that—opportunities that come from editors at the newspaper itself; from routine or unexpected events; from laws that guarantee the public access to government records and proceedings; and from sources, many of whom will want to expose sensitive information. And from your own imagination and curiosity about the way things operate.

Day-To-Day Activities

As a new reporter, you will often begin your day by gathering information on a subject about which you plan to write. Where do such stories originate?

An editor may assign you to cover a press conference at which the mayor will unveil the new city budget, which carries a major tax increase. While monitoring the city's police radio frequencies, your newspaper learns that a homicide has just occurred and sends you out. During your routine visit to the town planning and zoning office, you are tipped off that a major shopping mall developer has been asking questions about a wide stretch of undeveloped land in town.

Perhaps a local school has been cited for building code violations and your subsequent inspection of state and town records reveals a disturbing pattern of such violations. Or an attorney telephones you about a lawsuit he filed against a chemical company that, the attorney claims, has been exposing workers to dangerous substances.

The exact subject matter you will write about will depend to a great extent on the regular beat you are assigned to cover.

If you cover a town, you may be responsible for many areas, including town departments and policy-making bodies like the police department, planning and zoning commissions, the school board, the town council, and the mayor or other chief officer. You probably will be involved in covering town political elections and the townspeople themselves, writing feature stories on interesting personalities.

You could be a business reporter or a sports writer. Or a statewide specialty reporter, covering the environment, education, law enforcement, the courts, labor or state politics. Or cover the federal government, the Supreme Court, Congress, even the White House.

Such specializations will require you to develop an expertise in the area for which you are responsible. You will have to know how government departments operate and what laws pertain to them.

Learning How To Learn

Gathering information about some subjects is very easy. In the case of the mayor's press conference, for example, town officials probably will be eager to explain the spending package in detail...and community leaders and special interest groups will be eager to criticize it. You will have lots of information, some good quotes and a story that will appeal to just about anyone who uses city services and has to pay taxes.

Covering the homicide probably will be more difficult. Concerned about protecting evidence or scaring away suspects, police will release only the barest details. Neighbors, family members and co-workers may be too frightened or upset to talk. They may even react angrily to your questions, regarding them as ghoulish or insensitive.

Yet your editors will be pushing you to come up with an explanation for the crime, to learn about the victim's life and, if it isn't released, the cause of death. You probably will feel frustrated, even angry yourself, as you try to do a job in a hostile and often sad environment.

That is not the only problem you will face in your efforts to gather information for a story. Sometimes you will have to explore extremely complex issues.

And unlike the leisurely-written term papers you are used to producing for college courses, the report you'll have to prepare for today's or tomorrow morning's edition is probably due in a few hours...at most.

The Challenge Of Beat Reporting

When I was assigned to cover *The Hartford Courant's* consumer and utilities beat in 1986, I realized how challenging some issues can be. Suddenly, I found myself having to write stories about an electricity rate increase that had been proposed by the state's major power company. Due to the effect the increase would have on homeowners and businesses, the subject was page-one material day after day—an exciting prospect for any reporter.

Yet I found myself confronted with issues so complex and unfamiliar that they began to look frightening. Gathering the details and trying to interpret them was problematical enough; assembling them into a story that wouldn't send readers into a stupefied coma was the second challenge I faced.

It was even more difficult because I was new on the beat and had to familiarize myself with "utility jargon," a specialized vocabulary known only to a microcosm of utility officials, state and federal regulators, and a select group of Wall Street financial analysts.

It took hard work, but after examining and re-examining all the pieces and considering and reconsidering explanations from those on both sides of the issues, things began to finally come together. I suddenly began understanding those complex issues.

The Rewards You'll Cherish

That's when journalism is most exciting. I had used all my resources—my education, analytical abilities, patience and outside research—to break through a monumental barrier. And once I understood it all, I was able to examine the arguments made by both sides, interpret them, and ask the hard questions, the ones that readers would have asked if they had had the time to investigate and learn the way I had.

Through that process, I had learned a lot about how things operated, about things I never even knew existed. More importantly, it was not hypothetical, not something I was reading about in a book. I was participating as a member of the public, representing the public and its right and need to know.

Even more gratifying, your story may cause some change.

Finding Your First Reporting Job

As a reporter, you will have to use many skills. You will rely on your knowledge of math to calculate the percentage the city budget is increasing. You will rely on your understanding of politics and government when you cover elections. Your familiarity with basic physical science will help you write that feature on advances in fiber optics and telecommunications.

In fact, as you rely on what you've learned in high school and college, you will find that journalism courses are not the ones you'll rely on the most. Rather, you will depend most on what you've learned in all those general courses—art, literature, biology, history, math and other areas. It is that knowledge that will help you know what questions to ask and how to interpret the answers. Of course, good journalism courses will not only teach you the basics of writing and reporting, but also expose you to government, business and the whole spectrum of institutions that you will routinely encounter in your reporting.

Many reporters get their best journalistic training on weekly newspapers, where just a few weeks covering routine meetings, fires and police calls and writing simple features will teach you more than months of journalism classes. Weeklies are also a good place to start because they involve you in areas of newspaper operation that are less accessible to reporters on daily newspapers, where jobs are more specialized—you probably will be exposed to photography, graphics, page layout, copy editing, story assignments and editorial writing. When you finally are employed by a daily newspaper, that weekly newspaper experience will help you appreciate and work with the specialists in all those areas.

But even before you get to a weekly newspaper, you will need to have a good understanding of how a news story is written, and that is where those journalism courses will be vital. You also will need a good background in grammar and spelling. And if you know how to use of all those special reference materials in the library, you will save a lot of time trying to find sources.

Are You *Sure* You Want To Be A Reporter?

As in any job, you will wake up some mornings wishing you could stay home, especially when everyone else gets the day off because it's a holiday or there is a hurricane or snowstorm.

You will have to get used to being called to cover a late-breaking news story just when you were about to go home. If there is a competing newspaper in your town, you may find that you've been beat on a story by one of its reporters, and your editors probably will want to know why.

Although the responsibility and power you carry as a journalist can be gratifying, at times it also can make you feel uneasy.

You will constantly fight to get stories done on deadline and, at the same time, get the dozens of facts and names correct. You will have to make sure you have covered and explained both sides of each issue. And you will have to try to keep your stories objective, even though you may personally feel strongly about the subject. Sometimes it will be difficult to identify the sources giving you accurate information and those who shouldn't be trusted because of some special interest they have. And there will be times, just after the newspaper goes to press, that you will feel your blood rush as you suddenly remember something important that you forgot to include or that should have been verified.

Editors will be unforgiving if you make a mistake, particularly if it gets into print; they also will be unforgiving if you miss a deadline.

Editors will criticize your story, even if *you* think it's the best piece you've ever written. You will learn how to stand back and see the validity in that criticism. And you will have to learn to recognize criticism that is invalid. Sometimes you will feel like your whole sense of reality has been shaken.

You will have to work hard to be creative under pressure. Sometimes it will be difficult to know exactly how to write a story. In some cases, you will be able to describe personalities, the way people or things look, to play up humor or irony or portray emotions, touching your reader with great happiness or sadness. Other times, you will need to stick to the facts. There will also be stories that can be written either way.

You will have to intuitively recognize when you have collected enough information, then know what to use, what to discard, when to go back and ask more questions.

Despite all the things you have to know, despite the late hours, the tough deadlines and all the other pressures, journalism often will be just fun. For example, in 1986, another *Courant* reporter and I decided to test a new state law exempting meals under two dollars from state sales tax. What resulted was a week-long eating binge that included everything from pizza and ice cream to hamburgers and chicken. We tried to buy as many combinations of food items as we could, each combination adding up to less than two dollars.

We found that the law was so complex that fast food restaurants found it difficult to understand and follow. Our story inspired state lawmakers to change the regulations.

It is not easy to do everything and have fun, too, particularly in a busy newsroom crowded with reporters and editors all trying to meet their own deadlines. But if you *can* do it, if you can sit down after compiling and examining all the facts and write the right story, with the correct information, the proper tone and all within deadline, you will feel an incredible sense of accomplishment and satisfaction.

When you see your story in the newspaper, when you hear and see the reactions, when you think about all you have learned, you will wonder if there is anything else that can be so rewarding and self-fulfilling.

ANTHONY GIORGIANNI joined the *Courant* in 1984, after working as a reporter and editor for two weekly newspapers in his native Long Island, New York. He is a 1978 graduate of the State University of New York at Oswego.

The Hartford Courant, with a circulation of more than 226,000 daily and 308,000 Sunday, is by far the largest newspaper in Connecticut, the third largest in New England and about the 50th largest nationwide. It's also the oldest continuously published newspaper in the United States—its first edition was in 1764. It is owned by the Times Mirror Company, which also publishes several other major newspapers, including the *Los Angeles Times,* Long Island's *Newsday* and the *Baltimore Sun.*

3

Internships: Key Preparation
For Your Future In Journalism

Mary Kay Blake, Director,
Recruiting/Placement/Newspaper Division
The Gannett Company

How valuable is an internship to someone trying to get into journalism?

Let's put that question another way: How good a beginning do you want your career to have?

What A Newspaper Internship Will Do For You

Internships are invaluable. They can:

• Give you a chance to see what your chosen profession will be like, day-in and day-out.

• Provide you with experience in your chosen field even before you graduate into it.

• Offer a solid portfolio of published work you can show potential employers.

• Help you learn how to organize time and jug-
gle projects.

• Match you with a number of present and potential mentors, each of whom may contribute
to your professional growth. (Everyone in a
newsroom—not just your supervisor—can help
you learn about life on a newspaper.)

• Develop strong work habits and daily dis-
cipline meeting deadline.

• Connect you with editors and colleagues who
may choose to use their first-hand knowledge of
you and their contacts in the industry to help
you find a full-time job at graduation.

• Turn into a job. Many an intern has moved
right into a professional role—or graduated and
then gone into one—at the newspaper where he
or she interned.

Most of the young people I know who are being hired in
the newsrooms of daily newspapers these days have three
credentials: a degree in journalism (often combined with a
second major); extensive experience on campus publications
(usually but not exclusively the college daily); and at least one
newspaper internship.

It's possible, of course, to land a job without all three of
these bits of background; I suppose there even are people who
find that first job without *any* of them.

But you'll find the search a lot easier and the newspapers
that are interested in you a lot more numerous if you've prepared yourself for the profession in these three ways.

A Variety Of Internship Opportunities

What kinds of internships are there? Probably as many as
there are newspapers. Indeed, if one of the established formats outlined below doesn't fit into your schedule or the kinds

of newspapers you can connect with, see how creative you can be in devising a unique program of your own that you can present to an editor. It'll show your creativity and the kind of ingenuity that is always of interest to an employer.

Among the established types of internships are these:

Full-time professional newsroom work for a specified period: It's usually three months (or 12 weeks) and usually in the summer. But the stay can be shorter or longer, and it could be any season of the year. Some newsrooms now have an ongoing, year-round internship program, often set up through a local or regional college.

Part-time work for a specified period: This kind of program usually lasts a semester and involves 10-20 hours or newsroom work per week. Again, however, flexibility is a key factor and the hours could be fewer (generally not more) and the time period shorter or longer.

Rotating internships: These involve work in several news-room departments—two weeks in features, two weeks on the copy desk, two weeks in sports, etc. Some are very structured and allow for little or no deviation; more often, however, your interests help decide which areas you will work in.

Paid internships and credit internships: In the former, you work for a weekly or hourly wage. In the latter, you earn college credit for the experience. Some newspapers offer both kinds, usually dealing with local colleges on the latter and students from farther away (who have to then find and pay for local housing) on the former.

Pre-professional and professional internships: The latter involve reporting, editing and photography roles and usually go to students between their junior and senior years in college (though they *have* been landed by younger students or gradu-ates who want/need another credential or a bridge to a job.) The former usually are support roles and involve research work, support work, clerical work and newsroom exposure, but not usually at the professional level.

Finding One That's Right For You

Work with your school's placement office. Be persistent: Ask to be on interview lists for any possibilities. Write lots of letters on your own to as many newspapers as you can find. Include with your cover letter a clear and concise resume and 6-12 examples of your work (neatly presented—not scraps of paper cut and pasted).

Be sure to have a trusted friend or colleague proofread your resume and letter. I know editors who immediately toss aside any applications that contain typos, misspellings, incorrect names or, worst of all, misspellings of their own or their newspaper's names.

Be willing to look beyond the "name" newspapers—too many students already are vying for the scarce internship spots. Look for the good mid-sized newspapers (those under 100,000 circulation) where you will be an integral part of the entire operation. You'll get broader experience there anyway.

Start early—some newspapers select their summer interns by January 1st.

Be flexible. Make sure the newspaper knows that if summer isn't a good time for it to have you as an intern, you could arrange your schedule to work during another season. (More and more students are taking the option of summer school and winter internships, in order to be available when the openings are.)

Try for part-time or stringing work at daily (or even weekly) newspapers in your hometown or the area around your school. Sometimes such roles lead to internships; they at least will provide clips and contacts to use in further searches for a spot and demonstrate your eagerness to gain experience.

Work on campus publications—again, they provide helpful clips. And the experience helps show an editor that you can organize your time well enough to handle both classes and work.

And What To Do Once You Have

Even before you begin the job (or arrive in town if it's not your local paper), make sure you are reading *daily* the newspaper of whose staff you soon will be a part. Ask for a mailed subscription if you're outside its local area It will help you become familiar with the newspaper, its style and staff; it also should help you begin to learn about the town and get your work off to a faster start.

Be curious and aware. Don't limit your learning to the department(s) to which you're assigned—spend some of your off-time in other sections. See what happens in features. Check out a busy Friday night in sports. Learn how the copy desk works—and what happens to copy in composing. Ask to sit in on daily newsroom meetings or weekly editorial board sessions. Observing the kind of interaction that occurs there (or doesn't) can help you better understand the newspaper— and whether it's one you'd like to join once you graduate.

Take a slightly different route to work every day—you may spot story ideas you (and other staffers) otherwise would bypass. That kind of enterprise often leads to good reader pieces —and strong investigative ones.

Ask lots of questions. Ask your editors what they like (and don't like) about their work. Ask your colleagues what kinds of editors they like to work for. Ask both about other newspapers they've worked for—and what made those newspapers great or not so great.

Push for feedback. Learn from the comments. And ask for specific reviews of your work. Don't settle for "it's fine." An editor may not have a lot of time to spend with you daily. So try to find out what he or she liked (or didn't like) about your leads one day. Ask about your transitions the next day. And whether you sought enough sources or asked them the best questions the day after that. Bit by bit, you'll begin to learn the techniques and skills that separate the great journalists from all the others.

Offer to work on longer-range stories in between your regular assignments. There usually are five or ten minutes (or more) of "down" time every time you're waiting for someone to call you back or a clip to be culled from the library. Use that time to begin building the research and phone call blocks for another story—or several stories. Keep each in a separate queue or notebook; keep building on them bit by bit. You'll end your internship with more clips than those who sat around waiting for assignments and learn some very valuable time-management and juggling skills that are crucial to all good journalists.

Remember that an internship is much like your education: You will get out of it what you put into it in terms of effort, energy, enterprise and enthusiasm.

If you think it will be a good experience—and seek every opportunity to make it one and to grow in and from it—you will find every moment of it worthwhile, now and in your very promising future. If you wait for assignments, don't ask questions and don't seek out new areas to explore, you might as well spend your time and energy in another way.

And probably in another profession.

═══════════════════════════════════

MARY KAY BLAKE, 42, has worked in newsroom recruiting and news staff development roles for Gannett Co., Inc. for 12 years. For nine years before that, she worked in newsrooms as a copy editor and reporter. She is a graduate of the College of St. Francis in Joliet, IL (B.A. with honors in English).

Her current role includes overseeing an extensive college-recruiting program for Gannett. Mrs. Blake also coordinates the consideration of Gannett newsroom staffers for other positions in the company and leads the search for "outside" talent to bring into the group.

She is married to a journalist. Her husband George is editor and vice president of *The Cincinnati Enquirer* (also a Gannett newspaper).

4

Internship Listings: U.S. And Canada

The listings are pretty self-explanatory. Following the name, address and telephone number of the publisher or newspaper, we listed two items of information about each—the **Newspapers Published** by the publisher listed (or **Other Newspapers Published** if the listing is for a single paper) and the **Total Employees** at the paper(s)—full-time first; part-time, if any, in parentheses. This will give you an excellent idea of the relative size of the newspaper/publisher.

The rest of the information in each listing relates specifically to the internships each company offers:

Internship Contact: The specific person in charge of internships—if there are different contacts for different departments or for different papers we've indicated them.

Internships Offered: Salaried, non-salaried or some of each ("Both"). Where specific salaries, travel stipends, etc. are known, they were included.

Average Number Per Year: Just a note here—a "?" means they have internships available, but couldn't (or would not) hazard a guess as to an exact number.

Departments: in which internships are offered.

Applications Received—This will help you gauge the relative competition for internships at each paper. Applying to one that receives only 20 applications for the 10 internships it offers obviously gives you better odds than fighting the 50 applicants for another publisher's single internship.

Period of Availability and **Duration**—Specific seasons or months (summer, year-round, May-August, etc.) and approximate length of each internship (6-8 weeks, etc.).

Duties/Responsibilities: What you'll be doing if you accept an internship there, by department if available.

Qualifications: The level of education they prefer, specific majors, whether interviews are required, etc.

Application Procedure: Exactly what to send them.

Application Deadline: The last date they will accept applications (if they offer a number of seasonal internships, we have attempted to list the deadlines for each specific season). Whatever the deadline listed, we strongly recommend applying as early as possible.

Decision Date: When you will hear from them.

If any of the above entries is missing from a particular listing,, that's because we were unable to confirm that entry with the company itself. Rather than give you wrong or misleading information, we simply omitted it.

Before the detailed listings begin, there is one other list—newspapers in both the U.S. and Canada that were surveyed for this volume who told us they do not offer internships at all. We have listed these separately. This list is almost as valuable as the listing of those with internships. After all, knowing who to avoid contacting will help you target the right newspapers and utilize your time far more effectively.

Newspapers That Do *Not* Offer Internships

(C) denotes a Canadian agency

Arizona Daily Star
Asheville Citizen-Times
Brampton Times (C)
Brandon Sun (C)
Calgary Herald (C)
Caller Times
Cambridge Reporter (C)
Camden Chronicle-Independent
Cape Breton Post (C)
Chronicle-Herald (C)
Daily Bulletin (C)
Daily Free Press (C)
Daily Gleaner (C)
Daily News (C)
Daily Press (C)
Daily Racing Form (C)
Daily Star (C)
Daily Townsman (C)
Dallas Observer
Dannsha News (C)
Edmonton Journal (C)
Examiner (C)
Fort McMurray Today (C)
Guardian & Patriot (C)
Hamilton Spectator (C)
Herald (C)
Hub (C)
International Herald Tribune
Journal of Commerce
Journal Pioneer (C)
Kamloops Daily News (C)
Kitchener-Waterloo Record (C)
L'Acadie Nouvelle (C)
La Presse (C)
Le Devoir (C)
Le Droit (C)
Le Journal de Montreal (C)

Le Journal de Quebec (C)
Le Soleil (C)
Manchester Union Leader
Memphis Journal
Mercury (C)
Michigan Chronicle
Montreal Daily News (C)
Nashville Banner
New York Daily News
New York Post
New York Times
Northern Daily News (C)
Oakland Press
Oshawa-The Times (C)
Peace River Block News (C)
Providence Journal Bulletin
Record (C)
Reminder (C)
Review (C)
San Francisco Examiner
San Francisco Newspaper Agency
San Jose Mercury News
Schenectady Gazette
Standard-Freeholder (C)
Star (C)
Telegraph-Journal (C)
Times (C)
Times-News/Chronicle-Journal (C)
Toronto Star (C)
Vancouver Sun (C)
Wall Street Journal
Welland-Port Colborne Tribune (C)
Western Star (C)
Winnipeg Free Press (C)
Winnipeg Sun (C)
Yukon News (C)

Newspaper Internship Listings

ABILENE REPORTER-NEWS
P.O. Box 30
Abilene, TX 79604
915-673-4271

Total Employees: 250
Internship Contact: Betty Walden, Personnel Administrator
Internships Offered: Salaried
Average Number Per Year: 3-4
Departments: Editorial (2-3), Advertising (1)
Applications Received: 50
Period of Availability: Summer
Duration: 12 weeks
Duties/Responsibilities: Interns act as full reporters—"not just writing obituaries"—and get their own bylines. Will work in all areas—news, sports, living section, etc. Interns welcomed back after graduation.
Qualifications: College juniors preferred; seniors hired occasionally.
Application Procedure: Cover letter, resume and writing samples to contact; directly to editor for editorial.
Application Deadline: February

AKRON BEACON JOURNAL
44 East Exchange Street—Box 640
Akron, OH 44309-0640
216-996-3180

Total Employees: 650
Internship Contact: Barbara Dean, Employee Relations Director
Internships Offered: Salaried
Average Number Per Year: 5-10
Departments: Advertising, Editorial
Period of Availability: Year-round
Duration: 6 weeks
Duties/Responsibilities: Vary according to department.
Qualifications: No specific information given.
Application Procedure: In-person application is preferred; cover letter and resume accepted.
Application Deadline: Ongoing.

ANCHORAGE DAILY NEWS
P.O. Box 149001
Anchorage, AK 99514-9001
907-257-4200

Total Employees: 390

Internship Contact: Lou Ann Hennig

Internships Offered: Salaried

Average Number Per Year: 4 (minimum)

Departments: Editorial, Newsroom

Period of Availability: Summer

Duties/Responsibilities: Photography (1), Reporting (2), Copy editing (1)

Qualifications: No age requirement; must be able to write well.

Application Procedure: Send cover letter, resume and clips to contact.

Application Deadline: February

Decision Date: April—May

ANN ARBOR NEWS
340 East Huron Street
Ann Arbor, MI 48104
313-994-6989

Total Employees: 380

Internship Contact: Ed Petukiewicz, Editor

Internships Offered: Salaried

Average Number Per Year: 4

Departments: Newsroom, Journalism

Applications Received: 20

Period of Availability: Year-round

Duration: 3 months (summer); 4 months (school year)

Duties/Responsibilities: Interns do general assignment reporting. They are expected to be reporters who do not need (and, therefore, do not receive) a lot of "hand-holding." Almost all interns have been hired back full-time after graduation.

Qualifications: Summer—College juniors or seniors; extensive writing experience. School year—Usually limited to University of Michigan students (undergraduate and graduate).

Application Procedure: Send cover letter, resume, writing samples to contact.

Application Deadline: Ongoing

ARIZONA DAILY SUN
P.O. Box 1849
Flagstaff, AZ 86002
602-774-4545

Total Employees: 90 (45 F/T, 45 P/T)
Internship Contact: Rick Velotta, Managing Editor
Internships Offered: Non-Salaried
Average Number Per Year: 2
Departments: Advertising, Editorial
Applications Received: 30-40
Period of Availability: Summer
Duties/Responsibilities: General news and office work.
Qualifications: College seniors only.
Application Procedure: Send for application.
Application Deadline: December 1

ARIZONA REPUBLIC
See listing for Central Newspapers and Phoenix Newspapers

ASSOCIATION FOR EDUCATION IN JOURNALISM
NYU Summer Internship Program for Minorities
Institute of Afro-American Affairs, New York University
269 Mercer Street—Suite 601
New York, NY 10003
212-998-2130

Internship Contact: Sidique A. Wai, Program Coordinator
Internships Offered: Salaried ($200 minimum)
Average Number Per Year: 15-20
Departments: Newspapers, Magazines, Broadcasting
Applications Received: 100-200
Period of Availability: Summer
Duration: 10 weeks (35 hrs/wk)
Duties/Responsibilities: Once accepted into program, intern is placed with a participating company (e.g., *New York Times, Ms.* magazine, AT&T, etc.). Interns are also enrolled in a two-credit course, "Journalism and Minorities." Workshops and panels available.
Qualifications: Must be a minority; full-time college junior or senior with top academic standing. Educational interests in journalism.
Application Procedure: Send cover letter, resume, transcript, faculty recommendations (2) and application.
Application Deadline: Dec. 3 for letter of request; Dec. 17 for application.

ATLANTA JOURNAL
See Listing for Atlanta Morning Constitution

ATLANTA MORNING CONSTITUTION
72 Marietta Street—P.O. Box 4689
Atlanta, GA 30303
404-526-5699

Other Newspapers Published: Atlanta Journal

Total Employees: 5,900

Internship Contact: John Hull, Personnel Director

Internships Offered: Both

Average Number Per Year: 3-4

Applications Received: 50-65

Period of Availability: Summer

Duration: 8-10 weeks

Qualifications: College juniors or seniors.

Application Procedure: Letter and application to contact.

Application Deadline: December

AUGUSTA CHRONICLE
AUGUSTA HERALD
See listing for Morris Communications

BALTIMORE SUN
501 North Calvert Street
Baltimore, MD 21278
301-332-6000

Total Employees: 2,300

Internship Contact: Barbara Scott Jones, Personnel Manager

Internships Offered: Salaried

Average Number Per Year: 4

Departments: Newsroom

Applications Received: 20

Period of Availability: Summer

Duration: 12 weeks

Qualifications: College juniors or seniors—with (at least) a 3.5 GPA.

Application Procedure: Application required.

Application Deadline: December 1

THE BATESVILLE GUARD
P.O. Box 2036
Batesville, AR 72503
501-793-2383

Total Employees: 35
Internship Contact: Jo Cargill, Vice President
Internships Offered: Salaried
Average Number Per Year: 1
Applications Received: 10-15
Period of Availability: Summer
Duration: 3 months
Qualifications: College juniors or seniors.
Application Procedure: Send cover letter/resume to contact.

THE BAY TIMES
See listing for the Kent Group

THE BEACON-HERALD
108 Ontario Street—P.O. Box 430
Stratford, ON N5A 6T6
519-271-2220

Total Employees: 130
Internship Contact: Ron Carson
Internships Offered: Non-Salaried
Average Number Per Year: 1
Departments: Newsroom
Period of Availability: School-year
Duration: 3 months
Duties/Responsibilities: Intern will be working as a reporter.
Qualifications: College juniors or seniors with related majors.
Application Procedure: Call for an application.
Application Deadline: Ongoing

BEE PUBLICATIONS
5564 Main Street
Williamsville, NY 14221
716-632-4700

Newspapers Published: 9 suburban papers in the Buffalo area.
Total Employees: 85
Internship Contact: David Sherman, Executive Editor

Internships Offered: Non-Salaried
Average Number Per Year: 3
Departments: All
Applications Received: 30
Period of Availability: Summer
Duration: 12 weeks
Duties/Responsibilities: Vary according to department.
Qualifications: College juniors or seniors.
Application Procedure: Send cover letter/resume to contact.
Application Deadline: June 1

BOCA RATON NEWS
34 SE Second Street—P.O. Box 580
Boca Raton, FL 33482
407-395-8300

Total Employees: 200
Internship Contact: Chris Ledbetter, Managing Editor—Newsroom, Wendy Morrissey—other departments.
Internships Offered: Non-Salaried
Average Number Per Year: 1-2 (Newsroom)
Period of Availability: Summer
Duties/Responsibilities: Reporters—Will cover cities stories and other news.
Qualifications: No information supplied.
Application Procedure: Send resume and clips to contact.

THE BOSTON TAB
See listing for the Tab Newspapers

THE BRADENTON HERALD
102 Manatee Avenue West—P.O. Box 921
Bradenton, FL 33506
813-748-0411

Total Employees: 220
Internship Contact: Barbara Cashion, Personnel Director
Internships Offered: Both
Average Number Per Year: 2-3
Period of Availability: Summer
Qualifications: College juniors or seniors.
Application Procedure: Contact company for application.
Application Deadline: December 1

THE BROOKLINE TAB
See listing for the Tab Newspapers

BUCKS COUNTY COURIER TIMES
8400 Route 13
Levittown, PA 19057
215-949-4000

Total Employees: 600
Internship Contact: Joe Halberstein, Associate Editor
Internships Offered: Salaried ($250/wk)
Average Number Per Year: 6
Departments: News, Advertising
Applications Received: 30
Period of Availability: Summer
Duration: 12 weeks
Duties/Responsibilities: Each intern is assigned to specific area—sports, photography, features, etc.—and does hands-on work within the department. Will assist in housing and in getting jobs after graduation, although paper tries to hire back its interns.
Qualifications: College sophomores—seniors (heading into Masters program). Interview is required (begin around Thanksgiving).
Application Procedure: Send cover letter/resume/writing samples to contact.
Application Deadline: September—December
Decision Date: February 1

BUFFALO NEWS
1 News Plaza—P.O. Box 100
Buffalo, NY 14240
716-849-3434

Total Employees: 1,200
Internship Contact: Ralph Wray
Internships Offered: Salaried
Average Number Per Year: 20
Departments: Advertising, Editorial
Applications Received: 40-60
Period of Availability: Summer
Duration: 12 weeks
Duties/Responsibilities: Hands-on newspaper work. Interns are expected to take the place of vacationing staff.
Qualifications: College juniors with journalism background.

Application Procedure: Send cover letter/resume/writing samples to contact. Students are asked to come in for a "tryout" during winter or spring break.

Application Deadline: December 1

CALIFORNIA VOICE
See listing for Reporter Publications

THE CAMBRIDGE TAB
See listing for the Tab Newspapers

THE CANTON ENTERPRISE
See listing for the News and Observer Publishing Co.

CAPITOL NEWS SERVICE
1113 H Street
Sacramento, CA 95814
213-462-6371

Total Employees: 10
Internship Contact: Verna Kline, Bureau Chief
Internships Offered: Non-Salaried
Average Number Per Year: 25
Departments: Editorial, Political Science Research
Applications Received: 30-40
Period of Availability: School-year
Duration: One semester
Qualifications: College juniors or seniors.
Application Procedure: Send cover letter, resume and writing samples (preferably published clips) to contact.

CARY NEWS
See listing for the News and Observer Publishing Co.

CEDAR RAPIDS-MARION GAZETTE
500 Third Avenue SE
Cedar Rapids-Marion, IA 52401
319-398-8211

Total Employees: 430
Internship Contact: Michelle Wiebel, Employment Assistant
Internships Offered: Salaried
Average Number Per Year: 3-4
Period of Availability: Summer

Duration: 7-12 weeks
Qualifications: College juniors or seniors.
Application Procedure: Send cover letter/resume to contact.

CENTER FOR COMMUNICATION, INC.
570 Lexington Avenue—21st Floor
New York, NY 10020
212-836-3050

Internship Contact: Susan Toothaker
Internships Offered: Salaried
Average Number Per Year: 15
Departments: Public Relations, Fund Raising, General areas
Applications Received: 300
Period of Availability: School year; summer
Duration: Semester; summer
Duties/Responsibilities: Researching, writing, updating media lists and publicity work.
Qualifications: College student (any year); must work 2 days a week minimum.
Application Procedure: Send cover letter/resume to contact.
Application Deadline: Ongoing

CENTER FOR INVESTIGATIVE REPORTING, INC.
54 Mint Street—4th Floor
San Francisco, CA 94103
415-543-1200

Total Employees: 15
Internship Contact: Dan Noyes, Managing Director
Internships Offered: Salaried ($100/month stipend)
Average Number Per Year: 6-7
Departments: Editorial research
Applications Received: 70
Period of Availability: Year-round (typically Jan.-June, June-Dec., and some summers)
Duties/Responsibilities: Interns might follow a story for several months, doing research, reporting , etc., while working under a senior editor.
Qualifications: College (any year); career changers accepted.
Application Procedure: Send cover letter/resume/writing samples to contact.
Application Deadline: April 15; Nov. 15

CENTRAL NEWSPAPERS, INC.
307 North Penn
Indianapolis, IN 46204
317-633-9208

Newspapers Published: The Indianapolis News, Indianapolis Star (see separate listing for two prior) Arizona Republic, Phoenix Gazette (see listing for Phoenix Newspapers)

Total Employees: 1,600

Internship Contact: Harvey C. Jacobs, Editor

Internships Offered: Salaried

Average Number Per Year: 20

Departments: Editorial, Newsroom

Applications Received: 200

Period of Availability: Summer

Duration: 10 weeks

Duties/Responsibilities: Very structured program—duties are to be considered full professional assignments. Three classes per week—one writing, 2 seminars with outside speakers.

Qualifications: College junior or senior or college graduate—internship here is intended to be a bridge from school to a full-time newsroom job.

Application Procedure: Complete application (available from contact or at many colleges) requiring letters of reference, writing samples and an original editorial.

Application Deadline: March 1

Decision Date: April 1

CENTURY PUBLICATIONS, INC.
3 Church Street
Winchester, MA 01890
617-729-8100

Newspapers Published: A number of suburban weekly papers in Boston area.

Total Employees: 15

Internship Contact: William Finucane, Executive Editor

Internships Offered: Non-Salaried

Average Number Per Year: 15

Departments: Editorial

Applications Received: 30-40

Period of Availability: Year-round

Duration: 10-12 weeks

Duties/Responsibilities: No more than 15% "grunt work." Interns get involved in sports, features, obituaries, photo layout, copy editing, feature and hard news writing. Program is very flexible, allowing students to work in their areas of interest.

Qualifications: College juniors or seniors.

Application Procedure: Send cover letter, resume, and writing samples.

Application Deadline: Ongoing

CHARLESTON DAILY MAIL
See listing for Charleston Gazette

CHARLESTON GAZETTE
1001 Virginia Street East
Charleston, WV 25301
304-348-5105

Other Newspapers Published: Charleston Daily Mail

Total Employees: 400

Internship Contact: Don Marsh, Editor, or James Smith, Managing Editor

Internships Offered: Salaried

Average Number Per Year: 6-8

Departments: Editorial

Applications Received: 50+

Period of Availability: Summer

Duration: 10-12 weeks

Duties/Responsibilities: Writing and reporting. Interns are rotated from one beat to another—State House, court house, education, etc.

Qualifications: College students (at least sophomores) with journalism classes.

Application Procedure: Send cover letter, resume and three writing samples/clips to appropriate editor.

Application Deadline: January

Decision Date: Early Spring

CHARLOTTE OBSERVER
600 South Tryon Street—P.O. Box 32188
Charlotte, NC 28202
704-379-6597

Total Employees: 1,500

Internship Contact: Paul Connelly, Personnel Services Manager

Internships Offered: Non-Salaried

Average Number Per Year: 21-25

Departments: Editorial (10-12), Circulation (8-10), Marketing (3)

Applications Received: 500

Period of Availability: Summer (some school year, but for local schools only)

Duration: 8-12 weeks

Duties/Responsibilities: Editorial—Actual reporting; interns are expected to "hit the ground with their feet moving." Editors coach and counsel in weekly sessions. Some "hand-holding" the first week, after which interns are expected to be out on their own. Marketing—Hands-on work in all areas of department. Circulation—Work with district managers and carriers, work with collections, follow up complaint calls, etc.

Qualifications: College juniors or seniors with background appropriate to department.

Application Procedure: Send cover letter and resume (writing samples if Editorial) to contact. Marketing and Circulation internships are heavily recruited through minority colleges.

Application Deadline: Dec. 1—Editorial; April 1—others

Decision Date: Early Spring.

CHATTANOOGA NEWS-FREE PRESS
400 East 11th Street
Chattanooga, TN 37401
615-756-6900

Total Employees: 525

Internship Contact: Ray Marler, Director of Personnel

Internships Offered: Salaried

Average Number Per Year: 2-3

Applications Received: 30-40

Period of Availability: Summer

Duration: 7-10 weeks

Qualifications: College juniors or seniors.

Application Procedure: Send for application.

Application Deadline: December 1

CHICAGO SUN-TIMES
401 North Wabash Avenue
Chicago, IL 60611
312-321-3000

Total Employees: 1,700+

Internship Contact: Tom Sheridan, Assistant Managing Editor

Internships Offered: Non-Salaried

Average Number Per Year: 6

Departments: Editorial
Applications Received: 500+
Period of Availability: Summer
Duration: 10-12 weeks
Duties/Responsibilities: Work as regular reporter, out on stories; hands-on involvement. Particular areas vary from year to year—local reporting, copy editing, sports, photography, etc.
Qualifications: Previous internship preferred. Highly competitive; program often filled by top journalism students from local colleges. Career changers rarely chosen.
Application Procedure: Cover letter, resume and writing samples (preferably published clips) to contact.
Application Deadline: January 15

CHICAGO TRIBUNE
435 North Michigan Avenue
Chicago, IL 60611
312-222-4571

Total Employees: 4,000
Internship Contact: Ronald Williams, Employment Manager
Internships Offered: Salaried
Average Number Per Year: 3-5
Departments: Editorial
Applications Received: 40-50
Period of Availability: Year-round
Duration: 14 weeks (or one semester)
Qualifications: College juniors or seniors.
Application Procedure: Send for application.
Application Deadline: Jan. 8; Dec. 1

CINCINNATI ENQUIRER
617 Vine Street
Cincinnati, OH 45201
513-721-2700

Total Employees: 1,000
Internship Contact: Dennis Doherty, Deputy Managing Editor
Internships Offered: Salaried
Average Number Per Year: 10
Departments: Editorial
Applications Received: 50-60

Period of Availability: Summer
Duration: 8 weeks
Qualifications: College juniors and seniors.
Application Procedure: Send cover letter/resume to contact.
Application Deadline: December 1
Decision Date: Early spring.

CINCINNATI POST
125 East Court Street
Cincinnati, OH 45202
513-352-2784

Total Employees: 118
Internship Contact: Carole Philipps
Internships Offered: Salaried
Average Number Per Year: 3-4
Applications Received: 40-55
Period of Availability: Summer
Duration: 7-10 weeks
Qualifications: College juniors or seniors.
Application Procedure: Send for application.
Application Deadline: December 1

CLEVELAND PLAIN DEALER
1801 Superior Avenue NE
Cleveland, OH 44114
216-344-4500

Total Employees: 1,800
Internship Contact: Maxine Lynch, Assistant Managing Editor
Internships Offered: Both
Average Number Per Year: 12
Departments: Editorial (10), Reporting (1), Photography (1), Graphics
Applications Received: 50+
Period of Availability: Summer (12 weeks)
Duties/Responsibilities: Majority of interns act as full-time reporters and are assigned to a regular beat—city, sports, police, etc.
Qualifications: College juniors or seniors.
Application Procedure: Send cover letter, resume and five clips (photographers: send slides) to contact.
Application Deadline: March 1
Decision Date: March 31

THE CLOVER HERALD
See listing for the News and Observer Publishing Co.

COLUMBUS LEDGER-ENQUIRER
P.O. Box 711
Columbus, GA 31994
404-324-5526

Total Employees: 600
Internship Contact: Sam Jones, Managing Editor
Internships Offered: Salaried
Average Number Per Year: 4-6
Departments: All
Applications Received: 100
Period of Availability: Summer
Duration: 10 weeks (flexible)
Duties/Responsibilities: Students concentrate in areas of interest but are expected to sample various activities spending a week in: copy desk, photo lab, news and features, and writing. They are evaluated and are asked to fill out a report about the internship program before theirs ends.
Qualifications: Prefer college juniors and seniors who are highly motivated. High school students have been accepted and trained in the past, but not as full interns.
Application Procedure: Send cover letter, resume and samples. Application will be sent once these are received.
Application Deadline: March 1
Decision Date: May 1

COURIER-JOURNAL
525 West Broadway
Louisville, KY 40202
502-582-4614

Total Employees: 1,008
Internship Contact: Marvin R. Aubespin
Internships Offered: Salaried ($250/wk)
Average Number Per Year: 12
Departments: Varies—Graphics, Photo, Sports, Copy Desk, Reporting
Applications Received: 160+
Period of Availability: Summer
Duties/Responsibilities: Interns work a full work week, often irregular hours—days off not necessarily weekends. Will meet weekly with editors, reporters and company officials to become acquainted with wide range of

newspaper operations. Interns are treated as professional staff and work closely with intern director, a regular staffer who makes recommendations on how to sharpen writing, art, etc. skills.

Qualifications: Preference given to students who live or attend college in Kentucky or Southern Indiana. College students who have completed one year are eligible, though preference given to more advanced students. Seniors heading to graduate school are occasionally accepted.

Application Procedure: Application required.

Reporters, Copy Editors—Send typewritten letter (less than 500 words) telling why you want to be an intern, your ambitions and interests, and any journalism experience. Include statement about typing ability and note college years you have completed. Include 10 (max) published clippings—if no published clips available, send writing samples (nothing will be returned). Editors will choose candidates and they will be tested and interviewed over Christmas vacation.

Artists—Send portfolio including illustrations, cartoons, layouts and other examples of work—need not be published.

Photographers—Send portfolio including at least one picture story (plus contact sheets) and up to 20 single photos.

Photo Editors—Send resume and brief out-line of work experience relating to picture editing, layout and design. Portfolio of clippings helpful.

Application Deadline: November 14

Decision Date: March 1

THE DAILY DISPATCH
1720 Fifth Avenue
Moline, IL 61265
309-764-4344

Other Newspapers Published: Rock Island Argus

Total Employees: 250

Internship Contact: Russell H. Scott, Managing Editor

Internships Offered: Salaried

Average Number Per Year: 4

Departments: Editorial, Advertising, Promotion

Applications Received: 75-100

Period of Availability: Summer

Duration: 12 weeks

Qualifications: College sophomores or juniors preferred.

Application Procedure: Send resume, letter (and clips) to contact.

Application Deadline: February 1

Decision Date: March 15

THE DAILY JOURNAL
8 Dearborn Square
Kankakee, IL 60901
815-937-3300

Total Employees: 130
Internship Contact: Mark Gibson, Managing Editor
Internships Offered: Salaried
Average Number Per Year: 4
Departments: Editorial
Applications Received: 40-50
Period of Availability: Summer
Duration: 8 weeks
Qualifications: College juniors or seniors.
Application Procedure: Send cover letter/resume to contact.
Application Deadline: December 1

THE DAILY REVIEW
116 Main Street
Towanda, PA 18848
717-265-2151

Total Employees: 75
Internship Contact: Dennis Irvine, Editor
Internships Offered: Non-Salaried
Average Number Per Year: 3
Departments: Reporting, Editorial
Applications Received: 50
Period of Availability: Year-round
Qualifications: High school graduates.
Application Procedure: Submit letter (including detailed background), resume and clips to contact. In-person interview required.
Application Deadline: Year-round

DALLAS MORNING NEWS
Communications Center
Dallas, TX 75265
214-977-8222

Total Employees: 350
Internship Contact: R.E. Hass, Internship Consultant
Internships Offered: Salaried
Average Number Per Year: 20

Departments: Newsroom
Applications Received: 500
Period of Availability: Summer
Duration: 10 weeks
Duties/Responsibilities: Resumes are evaluated to see where students would fit best. Interns are then assigned to that beat/department and the editor in charge will assign duties.
Qualifications: College juniors and seniors.
Application Procedure: Send cover letter, resume, and (5-10) clips. Interns interested in photography should submit portfolio of photos.
Application Deadline: February 1
Decision Date: March 1

DALLAS TIMES HERALD
1101 Pacific Avenue
Dallas, TX 75202
214-720-6111

Total Employees: 1,400
Internship Contact: Tom Rice, Sr. VP-Human Resources
Internships Offered: Salaried
Average Number Per Year: 4-5
Applications Received: 40-50
Period of Availability: Summer
Duration: 10-12 weeks
Qualifications: College juniors or seniors.
Application Procedure: Send cover letter/resume to contact. Application will be required.

DAYTONA BEACH JOURNAL
901 Sixth Street
Daytona Beach, FL 32015
904-252-1511

Total Employees: 750
Internship Contact: Richard Kearley, Personnel Director
Internships Offered: Salaried
Average Number Per Year: 3-4
Departments: Journalism
Applications Received: 20-30
Period of Availability: Summer
Duration: 12 weeks

Qualifications: College juniors or seniors.

Application Procedure: Send cover letter/resume to contact.

Application Deadline: Early Spring.

DECATUR HERALD AND REVIEW
601 East William Street—Box 311
Decatur, IL 62525
217-429-5151

Internship Contact: Terri Kuhle, Personnel Manager

Internships Offered: Salaried (hourly wage)

Average Number Per Year: 2

Departments: Reporting

Period of Availability: Summer

Duration: 12 weeks

Duties/Responsibilities: Work as a staff reporter, filling in for those on vacation.

Qualifications: Strong writing background.

Application Procedure: Send cover letter, resume, and writing samples.

Application Deadline: February 1

Decision Date: February 15

DELAWARE COUNTY DAILY TIMES
500 Mildred Avenue
Primos, PA 19018
215-284-7200

Total Employees: 140

Internship Contact: Linda DeMeglio, Managing Editor

Internships Offered: Salaried

Average Number Per Year: 3

Departments: Editorial—Reporters: news (2), sports (1)

Applications Received: 50

Period of Availability: May-October

Duration: Up to six months.

Qualifications: College sophomores—seniors.

Application Procedure: Send cover letter/resume/writing samples to contact. In-person interview required.

Application Deadline: March 1

THE DESERET NEWS PUBLISHING CO.
30 East First South Street—P.O. Box 1257
Salt Lake City, UT 84110
801-237-2800

Other Newspapers Published: The Tribune

Total Employees: 165

Internship Contact: Keith D. West, Personnel Director

Internships Offered: Salaried ($5.00/hr)

Average Number Per Year: 8

Departments: City Desk

Applications Received: 40

Period of Availability: May-October

Duration: 3-6 months

Duties/Responsibilities: Writing and reporting.

Qualifications: College sophomores—seniors attending one of the three major Utah universities. Journalism skills/background required.

Application Procedure: Send cover letter/resume/writing samples to contact. In-person interview required.

Application Deadline: March 1

DES MOINES REGISTER
P.O. Box 957
Des Moines, IA 50304
515-284-8000

Other Newspapers Published: Indinola Register, Independence Newspaper

Total Employees: 1,150

Internship Contact: David Westphal, Managing Editor

Internships Offered: Salaried

Average Number Per Year: 20

Departments: All

Applications Received: 60

Period of Availability: Summer (primarily)

Duration: 12 weeks

Duties/Responsibilities: Will vary according to department.

Qualifications: College juniors or seniors.

Application Procedure: Send for required application.

Application Deadline: December 1

Decision Date: Varies

DETROIT FREE PRESS
321 West Lafayette
Detroit, MI 48231
313-222-6490

Total Employees: 2,000

Internship Contact: Kathy Warbelow, Managing Editor

Internships Offered: Salaried (union wages)

Average Number Per Year: 12

Departments: Editorial, Newsroom

Applications Received: 300

Period of Availability: Summer

Duration: Mid-May to September

Duties/Responsibilities: Assigned to various sections (e.g., city, sports, etc.); may be assigned to local bureaus.

Qualifications: College seniors (preferred); some juniors.

Application Procedure: Send cover letter, resume and writing samples. Interview with college recruiter will be arranged.

Application Deadline: December 31

Decision Date: End of February (can vary).

DETROIT NEWS
615 Lafayette Boulevard
Detroit, MI 48231
313-222-5420

Total Employees: 2,200

Internship Contact: Bob Taylor, Personnel Manager

Internships Offered: Salaried

Average Number Per Year: Varies

Departments: Newsroom

Period of Availability: Summer

Duration: 12 weeks

Qualifications: College sophomores—seniors and graduates.

Application Procedure: Send cover letter, resume and writing samples. Limited applications.

Application Deadline: December 1

DOW JONES NEWSPAPER FUND
Box 300
Princeton, NJ 08543
609-452-2820

Internship Contact: Jan Maressa, Office Manager

Internships Offered: Salaried ($1,000 scholarship to school on completion).

Average Number Per Year: 60

Departments: Reporting, Copy Editing

Period of Availability: Summer

Duration: 2 weeks training; 10 weeks work

Duties/Responsibilities: Interns are placed with major papers nationwide; paper participation varies from year to year, but examples are the *Chicago Tribune, Newsday, Los Angeles Times, Washington Post*, etc. There is a basic two week "crash course" after which duties will vary from paper to paper.

Qualifications: 10 internships (min.) in reporting for minority sophomores; 50 copy editing internships for college juniors.

Application Procedure: Must complete a 4-page application and a writing exercise. Send a cover letter, resume, writing samples, and two letters of recommendation to contact; or call for more information.

Application Deadline: November 15

Decision Date: By Spring Break.

DURHAM HERALD COMPANY, INC.
115 Market Street
Durham, NC 27702
919-687-6500

Newspapers Published: Durham Morning Herald, The Durham Sun

Total Employees: 500

Internship Contact: Sandra Gainey, Personnel Director

Average Number Per Year: 2 (per semester)

Departments: Library

Period of Availability: Year-round

Duration: One semester (12-15 hrs/wk)

Duties/Responsibilities: Student must keep log of internship experiences, meet at least four times with head librarian and complete a special project agreed upon by librarian, supervising professor and student. Intern receives thorough indoctrination into services and operations of a newspaper library.

Qualifications: Intern must be enrolled in accredited graduate library science degree program, have completed introductory library science courses, possess basic filing and typing skills (40 wpm min.), enjoy reading and be willing to do clerical tasks.

Application Procedure: Send resume to contact. Interview required. Intern must secure approval of supervising professor and register for course credit. Not an open application.

EMPIRE STATE WEEKLIES
2010 Empire Blvd.
Webster, NY 14580
716-671-1533

Newspapers Published: Webster Herald, Penfield Press, Fair Port-Punton Herald Mail, Wayne County Mail, Victor Herald, Soduf Record

Total Employees: 40

Internship Contact: James J. Gertner, Managing Publisher

Internships Offered: Non-Salaried

Average Number Per Year: 6 (two at a time)

Departments: Editorial, Advertising

Applications Received: 12

Period of Availability: Summer, Winter, Fall

Duration: 12 weeks

Qualifications: College sophomores—seniors.

Application Procedure: Submit cover letter and recommendation from your school professor or department head.

Application Deadline: Fall—Sept. 30; Winter—Jan. 30; Summer—May 30.

THE EVENING POST PUBLISHING CO.
134 Columbus Street
Charleston, SC 29402
803-577-7111

Other Newspapers Published: The News & Courier

Total Employees: 500+

Internship Contact: Howard McDougall

Internships Offered: Salaried ($225/wk)

Average Number Per Year: 7

Departments: Newsroom, Features, Sports

Period of Availability: Summer

Duration: 12 weeks

Qualifications: College sophomores or juniors.

Application Procedure: Send cover letter and resume. Application will then be mailed to you.

Application Deadline: Letter by January 31.

Decision Date: March 15

FAIR PORT-PUNTON HERALD MAIL
See listing for Empire State Weeklies

FAYETTEVILLE OBSERVER
458 Whitfield Street—P.O. Box 849
Fayetteville, NC 28302
919-323-4848

Other Newspapers Published: Fayetteville Times
Total Employees: 450
Internship Contact: John Holmes, Personnel Director
Internships Offered: Salaried
Average Number Per Year: 1-2
Applications Received: 10-15
Period of Availability: Summer
Duration: 8 weeks
Qualifications: College graduates only.
Application Procedure: Send cover letter/resume to contact.
Application Deadline: January 1
Decision Date: March

FAYETTEVILLE TIMES
See listing for Fayetteville Observer

FLORIDA TIMES-UNION
1 Riverside Avenue—P.O. Box 1949
Jacksonville, FL 32231
904-359-4111

Total Employees: 950
Internship Contact: Ron Martin, Managing Editor
Internships Offered: Both
Average Number Per Year: 11
Departments: All
Applications Received: 50-75
Period of Availability: Summer (for reporters), year-round (for photographers)
Duration: 8-12 weeks
Qualifications: College students.
Application Procedure: Send cover letter/resume to contact.
Application Deadline: December 1
Decision Date: Early Spring.

FORT WAYNE NEWSPAPERS
600 West Main Street
Fort Wayne, IN 46802
219-461-8444

Other Newspapers Published: The Journal Gazette, The News-Sentinel

Total Employees: 550

Internship Contact: Sherry Skufca

Average Number Per Year: 1-2

Departments: All

Applications Received: 10

Period of Availability: Summer

Duration: 8 weeks

Duties/Responsibilities: Will discuss.

Qualifications: College graduates.

Application Procedure: Send cover letter/resume to contact.

Application Deadline: December 1

Decision Date: Early Spring.

FORT WORTH STAR TELEGRAM
P.O. Box 1870
Fort Worth, TX 76101
817-390-7400

Total Employees: 1,200

Internship Contact: Jim Mason, Personnel Manager

Internships Offered: Non-Salaried

Average Number Per Year: 4

Departments: All

Applications Received: 10-20

Period of Availability: Summer

Duration: 8 weeks

Duties/Responsibilities: Vary according to department.

Qualifications: College juniors and seniors.

Application Procedure: Send cover letter/resume to contact.

Application Deadline: December 1

Decision Date: Mid-March

THE FRAMINGHAM TAB
See listing for the Tab Newspapers

GAINESVILLE SUN
2700 SW 13th Street—Drawer A
Gainesville, FL 32608
904-378-1411

Total Employees: 220
Internship Contact: Marty Paterson, Office Manager
Internships Offered: ?
Average Number Per Year: 3-5
Departments: All
Applications Received: 15
Period of Availability: Summer
Duration: 8-10 weeks
Duties/Responsibilities: Vary according to department.
Qualifications: College graduates.
Application Procedure: Send cover letter/resume to contact.
Application Deadline: December

GANNETT CO., INC.
1100 Wilson Boulevard
Arlington, VA 22209
703-284-6000

Newspapers Published: 83 daily (including *USA Today*), 35 non-daily (many are listed separately in this chapter; consult <u>Editor & Publisher Yearbook</u> for up-to-date listings of newspaper group ownership).
Total Employees: 37,000
Internship Contact: Mary Kay Blake, Director of Recruiting/Placement
Internships Offered: Both
Average Number Per Year: 400
Departments: All
Period of Availability: Year-round
Duration: Flexible
Duties/Responsibilities: Vary depending on department.
Qualifications: High school or college student.
Application Procedure: Send cover letter and resume to contact. The Gannett Company has locations all over the country—you may indicate geographic preference in your letter.
Application Deadline: Ongoing
Decision Date: No specific date for a decision, but acknowledgement of receipt will be made.

GANNETT ROCHESTER NEWSPAPERS
55 Exchange Street
Rochester, NY 14614
716-232-7100

Newspapers Published: Rochester Democrat Chronicle, Rochester Times Union

Total Employees: 1,100

Internship Contact: Patricia Rissberger

Internships Offered: Salaried

Average Number Per Year: 7

Departments: Editorial (6), Photography (1)

Applications Received: 50

Period of Availability: Summer

Duration: 10 weeks

Duties/Responsibilities: Generally work as staff reporters; may occasionally work as copy editors. Company might hire interns back for full-time positions; they have done this in the past.

Qualifications: College juniors and seniors.

Application Procedure: Send cover letter, resume, and writing samples to contact.

Application Deadline: January 15

Decision Date: March 1

GARY POST-TRIBUNE
1065 Broadway
Gary, IN 46402
219-881-3000

Total Employees: 81 (Newsroom)

Internship Contact: Al Johnson, Executive Editor

Internships Offered: Salaried

Average Number Per Year: 2-3

Departments: Newsroom

Applications Received: 15-18

Period of Availability: Summer

Duration: 13 weeks

Qualifications: College juniors, seniors or graduate students.

Application Procedure: Send cover letter/resume to contact.

Application Deadline: End of December.

Decision Date: February

GOLD LEAF FARMER
See listing for the News and Observer Publishing Co.

GRAND FORKS HERALD
120 North 4th Street
Grand Forks, ND 58201
701-780-1100

Total Employees: 250

Internship Contact: Mike Jacobs, Editor

Internships Offered: Both

Average Number Per Year: 4

Department: Reporting

Applications Received: 20

Period of Availability: Year-round

Duration: 12 weeks

Qualifications: College students.

Application Procedure: Send cover letter/resume to contact.

Application Deadline: December 1 (for summer).

GREENSBORO NEWS AND RECORD
200 East Market Street
Greensboro, NC 27420
919-373-7000

Total Employees: 112

Internship Contact: Ned Cline, Managing Editor

Internships Offered: Salaried ($275/wk)

Average Number Per Year: 8

Departments: Photography, News, Copy Desk, Production, Sports

Applications Received: 100

Period of Availability: Summer

Duration: 12 weeks

Qualifications: College juniors, seniors and graduate students.

Application Procedure: Send cover letter/resume to contact.

Application Deadline: March 1

Decision Date: Varies

HARRISBURG EVENING NEWS
812 Market Street—P.O. Box 2265
Harrisburg, PA 17105
717-255-8100

Total Employees: 515
Internship Contact: Mary Runkle, Personnel Manager
Internships Offered: Both
Average Number Per Year: 2-4
Departments: All
Applications Received: 40-50
Period of Availability: Summer
Duration: 6-12 weeks
Qualifications: College graduates only.
Application Procedure: Send cover letter/resume to contact.
Application Deadline: December 1

HOUSTON CHRONICLE
801 Texas Avenue
Houston, TX 77002
713-220-7171

Total Employees: 1,825
Internship Contact: Beverly Lumberg, Manager of Records
Internships Offered: Both
Average Number Per Year: 2-3
Departments: All
Applications Received: 10-12
Period of Availability: Summer
Duration: 6-12 weeks
Qualifications: College graduates.
Application Procedure: Send cover letter/resume to contact.
Application Deadline: December 1
Decision Date: March

HOUSTON POST
4747 Southwest Freeway
Houston, TX 77001
713-840-5600

Total Employees: 1,200
Internship Contact: Ernie Williamson, Executive Editor
Internships Offered: Salaried

Average Number Per Year: 3
Applications Received: 15
Period of Availability: Summer
Duration: 12 weeks
Qualifications: College graduates only.
Application Procedure: Send cover letter and resume.
Application Deadline: December 1

THE INDEPENDENCE
See listing for the Des Moines Register

INDIANAPOLIS STAR AND NEWS
307 North Pennsylvania Street
Indianapolis, IN 46206
317-633-9051

Total Employees: 1,700
Internship Contact: Harvey C. Jacobs, Editor—News
Internships Offered: Salaried
Average Number Per Year: 3-4
Applications Received: 40-50
Period of Availability: Summer
Duration: 6-8 weeks
Application Procedure: Send cover letter/resume to contact.
Application Deadline: December 1

THE INDINOLA REGISTER
See listing for the Des Moines Register

THE JERSEY JOURNAL
30 Journal Square
Jersey City, NJ 07306
201-653-1000

Total Employees: 50
Internship Contact: Judith Locorriere, Managing Editor
Internships Offered: Salaried
Average Number Per Year: 2-3
Departments: All
Period of Availability: Summer
Duration: 6-12 weeks
Application Procedure: Send cover letter/resume to contact.
Application Deadline: December 1

THE JOURNAL GAZETTE
See listing for Fort Wayne Newspapers

KALAMAZOO GAZETTE
401 South Burdick Street
Kalamazoo, MI 49003
616-345-3511

Total Employees: 293

Internship Contact: James Mosby Jr., Editor

Internships Offered: Both

Average Number Per Year: 2

Departments: Circulation, Display, Editing

Applications Received: 15

Period of Availability: Summer

Duration: 8 weeks

Duties/Responsibilities: Discussed upon acceptance.

Qualifications: College graduates only.

Application Procedure: Send cover letter/resume to contact.

THE KENT GROUP
A subsidiary of Chesapeake Pub.
P.O. Box 30
Chestertown, MD 21620
301-778-2011

Newspapers Published: Kent County News (Chestertown); Queen Anne's Record-Observer (Centreville); The Bay Times (Stevensville)

Total Employees: 12

Internship Contact: H. Hurtt Deringer, Publisher & Editor

Internships Offered: Salaried

Average Number Per Year: 1

Departments: Editorial

Applications Received: 10-15

Period of Availability: Summer

Duration: 7-12 weeks

Qualifications: College graduates.

Application Procedure: Send cover letter/resume to contact.

LA CROSSE TRIBUNE
401 North Third Street
La Crosse, WI 54601
608-782-9710

Total Employees: 126 (75 part-time)
Internship Contact: Meribeth Catania, Human Resource Manager
Internships Offered: Salaried
Average Number Per Year: 4
Departments: Newsroom
Applications Received: 25
Period of Availability: Summer (2), Fall (1), Spring (1)
Duration: 12 weeks
Qualifications: College sophomores—seniors, and graduates.
Application Procedure: Send cover letter/resume to contact.

LAS VEGAS REVIEW-JOURNAL
Box 70
Las Vegas, NV 89125
702-383-0289

Internship Contact: Charles Zobell, City Editor
Internships Offered: Salaried
Average Number Per Year: 4
Departments: Features (1), News (2), Photography (1)
Period of Availability: Summer
Duration: 10-12 weeks
Duties/Responsibilities: Hands-on reporting, feature writing, photography.
Qualifications: Junior journalism majors preferred, or seniors one semester short of graduation.
Application Procedure: Send letter, resume, writing samples and references.
Decision Date: March 15

THE LEADER-POST
1964 Park Street
Regina, SK S4P 3G4
306-565-8211

Total Employees: 400
Internship Contact: Managing Editor
Internships Offered: Non-Salaried
Average Number Per Year: ?
Departments: Journalism

Period of Availability: School year
Duration: One semester
Qualifications: College students.
Application Procedure: Call for an application.

THE LEADER-TELEGRAM
701 South Farwell
Eau Claire, WI 54701
715-834-3471

Total Employees: 250
Internship Contact: E. Ringhand, Editor
Internships Offered: Salaried
Average Number Per Year: 2-3
Departments: Editorial
Applications Received: 30
Period of Availability: Summer (12 weeks)
Qualifications: College students.
Application Procedure: Send cover letter/resume to contact.
Application Deadline: January 1

THE LEDGER
Box 408
Lakeland, FL 33802
813-687-7820

Total Employees: 275
Internship Contact: Bruce Giles, Managing Editor
Internships Offered: Salaried
Average Number Per Year: 2
Departments: Newsroom
Applications Received: 60
Period of Availability: Reporter—Jan. to April; Copy Desk—May to Aug.;
Minority internship—May to Aug.; Photographer—Sept. to Dec.
Duties/Responsibilities: Assist reporters, copy editors and photographers in
the newsroom—will receive hands-on experience.
Qualifications: College juniors or seniors preferred; will consider exceptional
sophomores.
Application Procedure: Send letter stating why you want an internship at
this company, as well as resume and clips or portfolio.
Application Deadline: Two months before desired date.
Decision Date: One month before start of internship.

THE LEDGER STAR
See listing for the Virginian-Pilot

LONG BEACH INDEPENDENT VOICE
320 East Park Avenue
Long Beach, NY 11561
516-432-0065

Total Employees: 3

Internship Contact: Terry Kohn, Managing Editor

Internships Offered: Flexible

Average Number Per Year: 4

Departments: Writing, Photography

Applications Received: 10

Period of Availability: School year

Duties/Responsibilities: General writing and proofreading duties. College credit may be arranged. If intern is not hired permanently after graduation, paper will assist in finding employment.

Qualifications: College students (at least sophomores with journalism courses); career changers and returnees to the work force considered.

Application Procedure: Send cover letter, resume, and recommendation from supervising professor. Interview will be required.

Application Deadline: At least one month prior to starting date.

LONG ISLAND JOURNAL
Box 697
Long Beach, NY 11561
516-889-1822

Internship Contact: John Gold

Internships Offered: Salaried

Average Number Per Year: 4

Departments: All

Period of Availability: Summer

Duration: 10-12 weeks

Duties/Responsibilities: Students get a chance to work in their area of specialization.

Qualifications: College juniors and seniors.

Application Procedure: Send cover letter/resume to contact.

Application Deadline: January 1

LOS ANGELES TIMES
A division of Times Mirror
Times Mirror Square
Los Angeles, CA 90053
213-655-8810

Total Employees: 8,000+
Internship Contact: Human Resources Director
Internships Offered: Non-Salaried
Average Number Per Year: 2
Departments: Publishing (Reporters)
Applications Received: 20-30
Period of Availability: Summer
Duration: 6-12 weeks
Qualifications: College graduates only.
Application Procedure: Send cover letter/resume to contact.
Application Deadline: Ongoing

MACON TELEGRAPH & NEWS
120 Broadway—P.O. Box 4167
Macon, GA 31213
912-744-4200

Total Employees: 380
Internship Contact: Ron Woodgeard, Managing Editor
Internships Offered: Both (see Availability)
Average Number Per Year: 8
Departments: Editorial
Applications Received: 50+
Period of Availability: Year-round
Duration: 12-13 weeks
Duties/Responsibilities: Interns are treated as regular reporters and are expected to be able to cover stories for publication.
Qualifications: College juniors or seniors.
Application Procedure: Send cover letter/resume/writing samples to contact.
Application Deadline: January 15
Decision Date: February 28

THE MARSHALL RECORD
See listing for the News and Observer Publishing Co.

METRO REPORTER
See listing for Reporter Publications

MIAMI HERALD
1 Herald Plaza
Miami, FL 33132-1693
305-350-2111

Total Employees: 4,000
Internship Contact: Mary Jean Connors, Managing Editor
Internships Offered: Salaried
Average Number Per Year: 15-20
Departments: Editorial (Reporters)
Applications Received: 400-500
Period of Availability: School-year
Duration: 12 weeks
Duties/Responsibilities: Interns are expected to do actual reporting. Those accepted into program have usually had experience in another internship program or as a stringer/correspondent on a local paper. Interns can be hired at end of program as full-time employees.
Qualifications: College juniors, seniors and graduate students.
Application Procedure: Send letter, resume and writing samples (published clips preferred and emphasized for qualifying).
Application Deadline: November 16
Decision Date: January

MILWAUKEE JOURNAL
Box 661
Milwaukee, WI 53201
414-224-2355

Total Employees: 2,000
Internship Contact: Paul Salsini, Staff Editor
Internships Offered: Both
Average Number Per Year: 40 (8 in newsroom)
Departments: Sports, Newsroom, Copy, Metro, Lifestyle, Entertainment
Applications Received: 380
Duties/Responsibilities: Will act as reporters.
Qualifications: Open to any undergraduate or graduate student.
Application Procedure: Submit letter, resume and writing samples to contact.
Application Deadline: December 31 (summer)
Decision Date: January

MOBILE BEACON
2311 Costaries Street
Mobile, AL 36617
205-479-0629

Internship Contact: Ms. Blackman, Personnel Department
Internships Offered: Salaried
Average Number Per Year: 1-2
Departments: Newsroom
Applications Received: 12-15
Period of Availability: Summer
Duration: 7-12 weeks
Qualifications: College graduates only.
Application Procedure: Send cover letter/resume to contact.
Application Deadline: December 1

THE MORNING ADVOCATE
See listing for the State Times

MT. OLIVE TRIBUNE
See listing for the News and Observer Publishing Co.

MORRIS COMMUNICATIONS
P.O. Box 936
Augusta, GA 30913
404-724-0851

Newspapers Published: Augusta Chronicle, Augusta Herald
Total Employees: 3,600
Internship Contact: Howard Eames, Executive Editor
Internships Offered: Salaried
Average Number Per Year: 4
Departments: Newsroom
Applications Received: 15-30
Period of Availability: Year-round
Duration: 10 weeks
Duties/Responsibilities: Interns are expected to do actual reporting and be able to write stories for publication.
Qualifications: College juniors returning to school for senior year only; must be journalism majors.
Application Procedure: Submit resume and writing samples to contact.
Application Deadline: March 1

NATCHEZ DEMOCRAT
503 North Canal Street—P.O. Box 1447
Natchez, MS 39120
601-442-9101

Total Employees: 55
Internship Contact: Judith Lott, Personnel Manager
Internships Offered: Both
Average Number Per Year: 2
Departments: Advertising, Editorial
Applications Received: 50
Duration: 12-14 weeks
Qualifications: College graduates only.
Application Procedure: Send cover letter/resume to contact.
Application Deadline: March 15

THE NATICK TAB
See listing for the Tab Newspapers

NATIONAL NEWS BUREAU
2019 Chancellor Street
Philadelphia, PA 19103
215-569-0700

Internship Contact: Harry J. Katz
Internships Offered: Both
Average Number Per Year: 16
Departments: All
Applications Received: 300
Period of Availability: Year-round
Duration: 12 weeks (or semester length)
Qualifications: Anyone with an interest in newspapers—i.e., English, writing, journalism majors. Will accept graduating seniors and photographers.
Application Procedure: Send letter, resume and writing (or photo) samples.

N. E. SENIOR CITIZEN
See listing for the Prime National Publishing Corp.

NEWARK STAR LEDGER
Star Ledger Plaza
Newark, NJ 07101
201-877-4141

Total Employees: 1,200
Internship Contact: Mark Herrick, Director of Sales and Marketing

Internships Offered: Salaried
Average Number Per Year: 2
Departments: Advertising
Applications Received: 40-50
Period of Availability: Summer
Duration: 4-8 weeks
Qualifications: College graduates only.
Application Procedure: Send cover letter/resume to contact.
Application Deadline: December 1

THE NEWPORT NEWS DAILY PRESS AND TIMES HERALD
7505 Warwick Blvd.—P.O. Box 746
Newport News, VA 23607
804-244-8424

Total Employees: 720
Internship Contact: Margaret Simonson, Human Resources Director
Internships Offered: Both
Average Number Per Year: 4
Departments: Newsroom
Period of Availability: Summer
Duration: 8 weeks
Qualifications: College seniors only.
Application Procedure: Send cover letter/resume to contact.
Application Deadline: December 1

NEWS AND COURIER
See listing for the Evening Post Publishing Co.

THE NEWS AND OBSERVER PUBLISHING CO.
2155 McDowell Street—P.O. Box 191
Raleigh, NC 27602
919-829-4500

Newspapers Published: The News and Observer, Raleigh Times, Smithfield Herald, Cary News, Yorkville Inquirer, Clover Herald, Canton Enterprise, Marshall Record, Mt. Olive Tribune, Gold Leaf Farmer, Zebulon Record.
Total Employees: 165
Internship Contact: Hunter George, Managing Editor
Internships Offered: Salaried
Average Number Per Year: 4
Applications Received: 30

Period of Availability: Summer
Duration: 10 weeks
Qualifications: College juniors or seniors.
Application Procedure: Send for application.
Application Deadline: December 1

NEWSDAY
235 Pinelawn Avenue
Melville, NY 11747
516-454-2020

Total Employees: 3,500
Internship Contact: Barbara Sanchaz, Editorial Personnel Manager
Internships Offered: Both (Spring/Winter—credit only)
Average Number Per Year: 40
Departments: Editorial
Applications Received: 400
Period of Availability: Year-round
Duration: 10 weeks
Duties/Responsibilities: Sophomores act as "aides"—typing, office duties, etc. Juniors/seniors act as reporters under guidance of editor.
Qualifications: College sophomores—seniors currently on school newspaper or who have worked at a local paper.
Application Procedure: Write for application in Sept. and include published clips.
Application Deadline: December 15
Decision Date: March

NEWSPAPER PRINTING CORPORATION
315 South Boulder Avenue
P.O. Box 1770
Tulsa, OK 74102
918-583-2161

Newspapers Published: The World, The Tribune
Total Employees: 800
Internship Contact: Edward Knighten, Director of Personnel
Internships Offered: Salaried
Average Number Per Year: 10
Applications Received: 50-60
Period of Availability: Three months.
Duties/Responsibilities: Will be assigned to an area of the newsroom; some

Duties/Responsibilities (Cont.): writing (10-15%), some "gofer" work.
Qualifications: College student.
Application Procedure: Send cover letter/resume to contact.
Application Deadline: April
Decision Date: May 1

NEWS PRESS
2442 Anderson Avenue
Fort Myers, FL 33902
813-335-0280

Total Employees: 600
Internship Contact: John Drunkenmiller, Executive Metro Editor
Internships Offered: Salaried ($250/wk)
Average Number Per Year: 6
Departments: All
Applications Received: 250
Period of Availability: Year-round
Duration: 12 weeks
Duties/Responsibilities: Hands-on experience in all phases of news work—reporting, writing small stories, paste-up, etc.
Qualifications: College juniors and seniors, plus career changers and those returning to work force.
Application Procedure: Send letter, resume and published clips to contact.
Application Deadline: September 1

THE NEWS SENTINEL
See listing for Fort Wayne Newspapers

THE NEWTON TAB
See listing for the Tab Newspapers

NURSINGWORLD JOURNAL
See listing for Prime National Publishing Corp.

OMAHA WORLD-HERALD
World Herald Square
Omaha, NE 68102
402-444-1000

Total Employees: 960
Internship Contact: Gene Overman, Personnel Manager
Internships Offered: Salaried

Average Number Per Year: 6
Applications Received: 50
Period of Availability: Summer
Duration: 8 weeks
Duties/Responsibilities: Vary according to department.
Qualifications: College juniors or seniors.
Application Procedure: Send cover letter/resume to contact.
Application Deadline: December 1
Decision Date: Varies according to number of applicants.

OREGONIAN
1320 SW Broadway
Portland, OR 97201
503-221-8280

Total Employees: 1,175
Internship Contact: Frank Lesage, Personnel Director
Internships Offered: Salaried
Average Number Per Year: 4
Applications Received: 70-90
Period of Availability: Summer
Duration: 9-12 weeks
Qualifications: College juniors or seniors.
Application Procedure: Send cover letter/resume to contact.
Application Deadline: December 1

ORLANDO SENTINEL
633 North Orange Avenue
Orlando, FL 32801
407-420-5000

Total Employees: 1,300
Internship Contact: James C. Clark, Deputy Managing Editor
Internships Offered: Salaried ($350/wk)
Average Number Per Year: 10
Departments: Newsroom, Photography
Applications Received: 250
Period of Availability: Summer
Duration: 12 weeks
Duties/Responsibilities: Assist in the newsroom; reporting, photography, paste-up and layout work.
Qualifications: College juniors and seniors.

Application Procedure: Send cover letter, resume and clips to contact.
Application Deadline: December 31
Decision Date: January

PACKET & TIMES
31 Colborne Street East
Orillia, ON L3V 1T4
705-325-1355

Total Employees: 45
Internship Contact: Jeff Day
Internships Offered: Non-Salaried
Average Number Per Year: 1
Departments: Newsroom
Period of Availability: School year
Duration: One semester
Qualifications: College sophomores, juniors, or seniors.
Application Procedure: Call contact for application. Be prepared to send resume.
Application Deadline: Ongoing.

PENFIELD PRESS
See listing for Empire State Weeklies

THE PENINSULA DAILY NEWS
Box 1330
Port Angeles, WA 98362
206-452-2345

Total Employees: 80
Internship Contact: Ken Fortinberry, Editing Department
Internships Offered: Salaried ($200/wk)
Average Number Per Year: 1
Departments: Newsroom
Applications Received: 50
Period of Availability: Summer
Duration: 13 weeks
Qualifications: College juniors or seniors.
Application Procedure: Send cover letter, resume and published clips to contact.
Application Deadline: March 15
Decision Date: Late June

PENSACOLA NEWS JOURNAL
1 News Journal Plaza
Pensacola, FL 32501
904-435-8591

Total Employees: 425
Internship Contact: James Barnett, Director of Human Resources
Internships Offered: Both
Average Number Per Year: 3-4
Applications Received: 60
Period of Availability: Summer (7-12 weeks)
Qualifications: College juniors and seniors.
Application Procedure: Send cover letter/resume to contact.
Application Deadline: December 1

PHILADELPHIA DAILY NEWS
North Broad Street
Philadelphia, PA 19101
215-854-5851

Total Employees: 175
Internship Contact: Brian Toolan, Assistant Managing Editor
Internships Offered: Salaried ($450/wk)
Average Number Per Year: 7
Departments: News, Photography, Features, Sports, Graphics, Copy, Business
Applications Received: 500
Period of Availability: Summer
Duration: 10 weeks
Duties/Responsibilities: All around assistance in newsroom, business office or copywriting departments.
Qualifications: College students or graduates; career changers; returnees to work force.
Application Procedure: Send letter, resume and clips or photos to contact.
Application Deadline: February 12

PHILADELPHIA INQUIRER
400 North Broad Street
Philadelphia, PA 19101
215-854-2000

Total Employees: 4,000
Internship Contact: Cynthia Murphy, Employee Programs
Internships Offered: Both

Average Number Per Year: 10-20
Departments: Editorial, Journalism
Period of Availability: Summer
Duration: 6-8 weeks
Qualifications: College juniors, seniors or graduates.
Application Procedure: Send cover letter/resume to contact.
Application Deadline: December 1

PHOENIX NEWSPAPERS
120 East Van Buren—P.O. Box 1950
Phoenix, AZ 85004
602-271-8000

Newspapers Published: The Phoenix Gazette, The Arizona Republic
Total Employees: 3,000

The Phoenix Gazette:

Internship Contact: Pamela Johnson
Internships Offered: Salaried ($324/wk)
Average Number Per Year: 4
Departments: News
Applications Received: 100+
Period of Availability: Summer
Duration: 13 weeks
Duties/Responsibilities: Three interns are hired as reporters, one as a photographer. Duties are to fill in for vacationing staffers. Reporters go on beats with the beat reporters, sit in at a city desk and work with feature writers.
Qualifications: College juniors or seniors with strong writing background.
Application Procedure: Send cover letter, resume and three clips to contact.
Application Deadline: January 1
Decision Date: February

The Arizona Republic:

Internship Contact: Bob Franken
Internships Offered: Both
Average Number Per Year: 5-10
Period of Availability: Summer
Application Procedure: Send cover letter, resume and writing samples.
Application Deadline: December 31
Decision Date: March

PITTSBURGH POST GAZETTE
566 Boulevard of the Allies
Pittsburgh, PA 15222
412-263-1524

Total Employees: 150
Internship Contact: John B. Craig, Jr., Editor
Internships Offered: Salaried ($359/wk)
Average Number Per Year: 6
Departments: Editorial
Applications Received: 300
Period of Availability: Year-round
Duration: 12 weeks
Duties/Responsibilities: Will discuss.
Qualifications: College juniors, career changers, people re-entering work force.
Application Procedure: Send letter, resume and writing samples to contact.
Application Deadline: December 31 (summer)

THE PRESS-TELEGRAM
604 Pine Avenue
Long Beach, CA 90844
213-435-1161

Total Employees: 700
Internship Contact: David Whiting
Internships Offered: Salaried
Average Number Per Year: 3
Applications Received: 25-30
Period of Availability: Summer
Duration: 12 weeks
Qualifications: College students or graduates.
Application Procedure: Send cover letter/resume to contact.
Application Deadline: December

PRIME NATIONAL PUBLISHING CORPORATION
470 Boston Post Road
Weston, MA 02193
617-899-2702

Newspapers Published: N.E. Senior Citizen, Senior American News, Nursingworld Journal, P.T.O.T. Job News
Total Employees: 30

Internship Contact: William Haslam, General Manager
Internships Offered: ?
Average Number Per Year: 1
Departments: Newsroom
Applications Received: 15
Period of Availability: Summer
Duration: 8-12 weeks
Qualifications: College student (any year).
Application Procedure: Send cover letter/resume to contact.
Application Deadline: Ongoing

PROVIDENCE JOURNAL-BULLETIN
75 Fountain Street
Providence, RI 02902
401-277-7500

Total Employees: 2,000
Internship Contact: Donald Zimmerman, Assistant Director, Personnel and Labor Relations
Internships Offered: Salaried (Comp. Science—$354/wk; News—$384/wk; Advertising—$402/wk)
Average Number Per Year: 23
Departments: News, Computer Systems, Advertising
Applications Received: 500
Period of Availability: Summer
Duration: Flexible
Duties/Responsibilities:

News: Interns may be assigned to day or night city staff, suburban news bureaus or Sunday department where work is done under close supervision of the professional staff.

Advertising: Program includes orientation program and hands-on experience in outside sales, telephone sales, research and support services.

Computer Science: Assignments are made on the basis of interest and experience. Past assignments have included programming in "C," an IBM Assembler, COBOL, MANTIS, and in a report generation language. Tasks have included assistance with News investigative reporting assignments, participation in coding 10,000 plus line page layout system, database applications, business graphics and communications problems.

Qualifications:

News: College sophomores or juniors; journalism major not required. College seniors and graduate students returning to school in the Fall will be considered.

Advertising: College juniors preferred; must be advertising or marketing major and member of the advertising sales staff of a self-supporting campus daily.

Computer Science: Undergraduates or recent graduates planning to attend graduate school in the Fall. Computer Science majors preferred.

Application Procedure: Submit cover letter, resume and transcript to contact (News—also send clips).

Application Deadline: January 15

Decision Date: March 1

P. T. O. T. JOB NEWS
See listing for Prime National Publishing Corporation

QUEEN ANNE'S RECORD-OBSERVER
See listing for The Kent Group

THE RALEIGH TIMES
See listing for The News and Observer Publishing Company

REPORTER PUBLICATIONS
1366 Turk Street
San Francisco, CA 94115
415-931-5778

Newspapers Published: California Voice, Sun Reporter, Metro Reporter Group (San Francisco, Peninsula/San Jose, San Joaquin, Oakland, Berkeley, Richmond, Vallejo)

Total Employees: 37

Internship Contact: Amelia Ashley-Ward, Managing Editor

Internships Offered: Salaried (stipend)

Average Number Per Year: 4

Departments: All

Period of Availability: Summer (2), Winter (2)

Duration: 12 weeks (summer); 4 weeks (winter)

Duties/Responsibilities: Hands-on reporting. Interns are sometimes even assigned to a pool in which they report and work for all of the papers.

Qualifications: College juniors with experience on college paper.

Application Procedure: Send cover letter, resume and clips to contact.

Application Deadline: One semester prior to starting date.

REPORTERS COMMITTEE FOR
FREEDOM OF THE PRESS
800 18th Street NW—Suite 300
Washington, DC 20006
202-466-6312

Internship Contact: Rebecca Dougherty

Internships Offered: Salaried ($750 stipend for full-time interns)

Average Number Per Year: 3 (full- and part-time available)

Departments: Reporting, Editing

Period of Availability: Year-round

Duration: 12 weeks

Duties/Responsibilities: To be discussed.

Qualifications: College students with journalism majors.

Application Procedure: Letter, resume and writing samples to contact.

Application Deadline: Summer—Jan. 31; Fall—March 31; Spring—Oct. 31.

Decision Date: Varies according to number of applicants.

RICHMOND NEWS INC.
333 East Grace Street—P.O. Box C-32333
Richmond, VA 23293
804-649-6000

Newspapers Published: Richmond News Leader, Richmond Times Dispatch

Total Employees: 1,500

Internship Contact: Managing Editor

Internships Offered: Salaried

Average Number Per Year: 12

Departments: Newsroom

Applications Received: 100+

Period of Availability: Summer

Duration: 12 weeks

Qualifications: College sophomores—seniors.

Application Procedure: Contact Mr. MacDonald in Personnel for application.

Application Deadline: January 1

Decision Date: Early Spring

ROANOKE TIMES & WORLD-NEWS
201-09 West Campbell Avenue
P.O. Box 2491
Roanoke, VA 24010
703-981-3100

Total Employees: 650
Internship Contact: News—William K. Warren, Managing Editor; Advertising—Judy Perfater, Advertising Manager
Internships Offered: Salaried
Average Number Per Year: 4
Departments: Editorial, Advertising
Applications Received: 25
Period of Availability: Summer (8-10 weeks)
Qualifications: College students or graduates.
Application Procedure: Send cover letter/resume to contact.
Application Deadline: December 1

ROCHESTER DEMOCRAT & CHRONICLE
See listing for Gannett Rochester Newspapers

ROCHESTER TIMES UNION
See listing for Gannett Rochester Newspapers

ROCK ISLAND ARGUS
See listing for the Daily Dispatch

ROCKY MOUNTAIN NEWS
400 West Colfax Avenue—P.O. Box 719
Denver, CO 80204
303-892-5000

Total Employees: 1,410
Internship Contact: Don Livingston, Employee Relations Director
Internships Offered: Both
Average Number Per Year: 1-2
Departments: Editorial
Applications Received: 10-15
Period of Availability: Summer
Duration: 8-12 weeks
Qualifications: College juniors and seniors.
Application Procedure: Send cover letter/resume to contact.
Application Deadline: January

ST. LOUIS POST-DISPATCH
900 North Tucker Blvd.
St Louis, MO 63101
314-622-7000

Total Employees: 1,600
Internship Contact: David Lipman, Managing Editor
Internships Offered: Salaried
Average Number Per Year: 1-2
Departments: Newsroom
Applications Received: 12-15
Period of Availability: Summer
Duration: 8 weeks
Qualifications: Minority scholarship program.
Application Procedure: Send cover letter/resume to contact.
Application Deadline: December 1

ST PAUL PRESS DISPATCH
345 Cedar Street
St. Paul, MN 55101
612-222-5011

Total Employees: 900
Internship Contact: Mary Newman, Human Resources Rep.
Internships Offered: Salaried
Average Number Per Year: 5
Departments: Editorial, Advertising, Circulation
Applications Received: 20
Period of Availability: Summer
Duration: 8-12 weeks
Qualifications: College juniors, seniors and graduates.
Application Procedure: Send cover letter/resume to contact.
Application Deadline: December 1
Decision Date: March 1

ST. PETERSBURG TIMES INDEPENDENCE
P.O. Box 1121
St Petersburg, FL 33731
813-893-8111

Total Employees: 3,000
Internship Contact: Ray Long, Employment Manager
Internships Offered: Salaried

Average Number Per Year: 20-25
Departments: Journalism, Business, Advertising, Production
Applications Received: 250+
Period of Availability: Summer
Duration: 12 weeks
Duties/Responsibilities: Journalism—Act as reporters or copy editors. Reporters might fill in for vacationing staffers and may even have their own beats. Interns in other departments fill in where necessary, but are given as much hands-on experience as possible.
Qualifications: College juniors and seniors.
Application Procedure: Send cover letter and resume to contact (plus writing samples for Journalism).
Application Deadline: November 15
Decision Date: December 15

SAN ANTONIO EXPRESS/NEWS
P.O. Box 2171
San Antonio, TX 78297
512-225-7411

Total Employees: 983
Internship Contact: Willis Moss
Internships Offered: Salaried
Average Number Per Year: 2
Departments: Editorial, Advertising
Applications Received: 25
Period of Availability: Summer
Duration: 8 weeks
Qualifications: College sophomores, juniors, seniors and graduates.
Application Procedure: Send cover letter/resume to contact.
Application Deadline: December 1

SAN ANTONIO LIGHT
420 Broadway
San Antonio, TX 78205
512-271-2971

Total Employees: 850
Internship Contact: Ed Rademaekers, Executive Editor
Internships Offered: Salaried
Average Number Per Year: 2-3
Applications Received: 10-15

Period of Availability: Summer
Duration: 8 weeks
Qualifications: College juniors, seniors or graduates.
Application Procedure: Send cover letter/resume to contact.
Application Deadline: December

SAN FRANCISCO BAY GUARDIAN
2700 19th Street
San Francisco, CA 94110
415-824-7660

Internship Contact: Heather Mackey, Editorial Assistant
Internships Offered: Non-Salaried
Average Number Per Year: 6-8 (4 times a year)
Departments: Editorial, Publishing
Period of Availability: Year-round
Duration: 3 months
Duties/Responsibilities: Editorial—Some clerical and writing, but mostly research. Publishing Asst.—Various duties, as needed.
Qualifications: Word processing experience required.
Application Procedure: Send resume, cover letter and writing samples.
Application Deadline: Ongoing
Decision Date: Will respond as positions are needed.

SAN JOSE MERCURY NEWS
750 Ridder Park Drive
San Jose, CA 95190
408-920-5000

Total Employees: 1,500
Internship Contact: Patty Fisher, Assistant Managing Editor
Internships Offered: Salaried
Average Number Per Year: 3-4
Applications Received: 15-25
Period of Availability: Summer
Duration: 8-12 weeks
Qualifications: College students or graduates.
Application Procedure: Send for application.
Application Deadline: December

SEATTLE TIMES
Fairview Avenue North—P.O. Box 70
Seattle, WA 98121l
206-464-2392

Total Employees: 2,000
Internship Contact: Rene Follett, Training Manager
Internships Offered: Salaried
Average Number Per Year: 1-2
Applications Received: 10-15
Period of Availability: Summer
Duration: 10-12 weeks
Qualifications: College sophomores—seniors.
Application Procedure: Send cover letter/resume to contact.
Application Deadline: December

SENIOR AMERICAN NEWS
See listing for Prime National Publishing Corp.

SMITHFIELD HERALD
See listing for the News and Observer Publishing Co.

SODUF RECORD
See listing for Empire State Weeklies

SOUTH BEND TRIBUNE
225 West Colfax Road
South Bend, IN 46626
219-233-6161

Total Employees: 500
Internship Contact: Ed Henry, Personnel
Internships Offered: Salaried
Average Number Per Year: 15
Departments: Newsroom (9), Advertising (6)
Applications Received: 50
Period of Availability: Summer
Duration: May—September
Duties/Responsibilities:

Advertising—Assist throughout department.

News—1 news photographer, 1 graphic design/ layout person, 1-2 copy desk, balance reporters. Reporters are "broken in" but are expected to be out on their own before the summer is over.

Qualifications: College sophomores and juniors preferred (will consider others). Experience in campus journalism important. Must have reasonable background of basic news writing, leads, etc. Good general academic background plus journalism courses.

Application Procedure:

Newsroom—Send cover letter, resume and writing samples to Mr. Powers.

Advertising—Send cover letter and resume to Mr. Ed Henry, Personnel.

Application Deadline: January 31

SPRINGFIELD NEWS LEADER
6512 Boonville Avenue
Springfield, MO 65801
417-836-1100

Total Employees: 350
Internship Contact: Jan Lowe, Human Resources Director
Internships Offered: Non-Salaried
Average Number Per Year: 4
Departments: Retail, Circulation
Applications Received: 40
Period of Availability: Summer
Duration: 8 weeks
Qualifications: College juniors and seniors.
Application Procedure: Send cover letter/resume to contact.
Application Deadline: Ongoing

STAR-NEWS
525 East Colorado Boulevard
Pasadena, CA 91109
818-578-6300

Total Employees: 195
Internship Contact: Jackie Knowles, City Editor
Internships Offered: Both
Average Number Per Year: 3-5
Applications Received: 40-45
Period of Availability: Summer
Duration: 8-10 weeks
Qualifications: College juniors or seniors.
Application Procedure: Contact company for application.

THE STATE-TIMES
P.O. Box 588
Baton Rouge, LA 70821-0588
504-383-1111

Other Newspapers Published: Morning Advocate, Sunday Advocate
Total Employees: 670
Internship Contact: Betty Jo Baker, Personnel Manager
Internships Offered: Salaried
Average Number Per Year: 2-3
Departments: Reporters
Applications Received: 20
Period of Availability: Year-round
Duration: 8 weeks
Qualifications: College juniors and seniors.
Application Procedure: Send for application.
Application Deadline: December

THE SUDBURY TAB
See listing for the Tab Newspapers

THE SUNDAY ADVOCATE
See listing for the State-Times

THE SUN REPORTER
See listing for Reporter Publications

THE TAB NEWSPAPERS
1254 Chestnut Street
Newton, MA 02164
617-969-0340

Newspapers Published: The Brookline Tab, The Newton Tab, The Boston Tab, The Cambridge Tab, The Wellesley Tab, The Natick Tab, The Weston Tab, The Framingham Tab, The Wayland Tab and The Sudbury Tab.
Total Employees: 180
Internship Contact: Kathleen Tesoriero, Personnel Coordinator
Internships Offered: Both
Average Number Per Year: Up to 10 (5 in Editorial)
Departments: Paste-up, Editorial, etc.
Period of Availability: Year-round
Duties/Responsibilities: Vary according to department.
Qualifications: College students (any year) or graduates.

Application Procedure: Send for application; attach cover letter and resume.
Application Deadline: December

TALLAHASSEE DEMOCRAT
277 North Magnolia Drive
P.O. Box 990
Tallahassee, FL 32302
904-599-2100

Total Employees: 280
Internship Contact: Doris Dunlap, Dir. of Employment & Community Relations
Internships Offered: Salaried
Average Number Per Year: 3-4
Departments: Where needed.
Applications Received: 25
Period of Availability: Summer (10 weeks)
Qualifications: College juniors and seniors.
Application Procedure: Send for application.
Application Deadline: December

TAMPA TRIBUNE-TIMES
202 Parker Street
Tampa, FL 33601
813-272-7711

Total Employees: 1,200
Internship Contact: Sandra Sheffield, Personnel Manager
Internships Offered: Salaried
Average Number Per Year: 3-4
Applications Received: 15-20
Period of Availability: Summer (10 weeks)
Qualifications: College juniors and seniors.
Application Procedure: Send for application.
Application Deadline: December

TOLEDO BLADE
541 Superior Street
Toledo, OH 43660
419-245-6163

Total Employees: 140
Internship Contact: Cheryl Lutz, Assistant Managing Editor
Internships Offered: Salaried

Average Number Per Year: 6
Departments: City Desk
Applications Received: 200
Period of Availability: Summer
Duration: 12 weeks
Duties/Responsibilities: General assignment reporting and clerical duties.
Qualifications: College juniors, seniors or graduate students.
Application Procedure: Send cover letter, resume and clips to contact.
Application Deadline: 3 months prior to internship period.

TRENTONIAN
Southard at Perry Street
Trenton, NJ 08602
609-989-7800

Total Employees: 250
Internship Contact: Emil Slaboda, Editor
Internships Offered: Non-Salaried
Average Number Per Year: 2-4
Applications Received: 20-40
Period of Availability: Summer
Duration: 8 weeks
Qualifications: College sophomores—seniors.
Application Procedure: Send for application.

THE TRIBUNE
See listing for Newspaper Printing Corporation

THE TRIBUNE (Salt Lake City, UT)
See listing for Deseret News Publishing Co.

USA TODAY
See listing for Gannett Co., Inc.

VICTOR HERALD
See listing for Empire State Weeklies

THE VILLAGE VOICE
842 Broadway
New York, NY 10003
212-475-3300

Total Employees: 250
Internship Contact: Lisa Kennedy, Asst. to Editor (ext. 509)

Internships Offered: Salaried
Average Number Per Year: 4
Applications Received: 40
Period of Availability: Summer
Duration: 8 weeks
Duties/Responsibilities: Vary according to department.
Qualifications: College sophomores—seniors.
Application Procedure: Send for application.

VIRGINIAN-PILOT
150 West Brambleton—P.O. Box 449
Norfolk, VA 23501
804-446-2385

Other Newspapers Published: The Ledger Star
Total Employees: 1,250 (plus part-timers)
Internship Contact: News—Ed Rogers, Assistant Managing Editor. All others—Ken Wyatt, Head of Personnel
Internships Offered: Salaried
Average Number Per Year: 16-18
Departments: Newsroom, Advertising, Circulation and/or Production
Applications Received: 200+
Period of Availability: Summer
Duration: 12-16 weeks
Duties/Responsibilities: The purpose of all internships is for students to get a chance to actually practice what they've learned in the classroom. In News, that means actual reporting and writing.
Qualifications: Most news interns recruited by Mr. Rogers are from the University of Missouri School of Journalism. Interns are usually between their junior and senior years in college, although both younger students and first- and second-year MBA candidates have been accepted.
Application Procedure: News—Cover letter, resume and writing samples to Ed Rogers; Other departments—letter and resume to Ken Wyatt.
Application Deadline: February 1

THE WASHINGTON POST
1150 15th Street NW
Washington, DC 20071
202-334-6000

Total Employees: 4,000
Internship Contact: Molly Yood, News Personnel Administrator
Internships Offered: Salaried

Average Number Per Year: 20
Departments: Newsroom
Applications Received: 500+
Period of Availability: Summer
Duration: 12 weeks
Duties/Responsibilities: Work in either reporting or copy editing. Reporters are given their own beat for the summer.
Qualifications: College juniors or seniors with strong writing background.
Application Procedure: Formal application is available by the end of August. A 500-word autobiography (part of application) must be submitted, as well as at least six news clips.
Application Deadline: November 15
Decision Date: End of January

THE WASHINGTON TIMES
3600 New York Avenue NE
Washington, DC 20002
202-636-3100

Total Employees: 1,000
Internship Contact: Terry Ott, Employment Manager
Internships Offered: Salaried
Average Number Per Year: 12
Departments: Editorial (8 in features or city desk), Sports, Photography
Applications Received: 250
Period of Availability: Year-round; more positions available during summer.
Duration: 12 weeks
Duties/Responsibilities: Hands-on writing; will see bylines in paper before end of summer.
Qualifications: College sophomores—seniors who are actively involved with their college newspaper and want to pursue a career in journalism.
Application Procedure: Send cover letter/resume/writing samples to contact.
Application Deadline: January 31 (summer)

THE WAYLAND TAB
See listing for the Tab Newspapers

WAYNE COUNTY MAIL
See listing for Empire State Weeklies

WEBSTER HERALD
See listing for Empire State Weeklies

THE WELLESLEY TAB
See listing for the Tab Newspapers

THE WESTON TAB
See listing for the Tab Newspapers

WHIG-STANDARD
306 King Street East
Kingston, ON K7L 4Z7
613-544-5000

Total Employees: 200
Internship Contact: Sheldon McNeil
Internships Offered: Non-Salaried
Average Number Per Year: 2
Departments: Newsroom
Period of Availability: School year
Duration: One semester
Qualifications: College juniors or seniors.
Application Procedure: Send cover letter/resume to contact.
Application Deadline: Ongoing

WICHITA EAGLE-BEACON
825 East Douglas—P.O. Box 820
Wichita, KS 67201
316-268-6000

Total Employees: 750 (including part-timers)
Internship Contact: James P. Spangler, Director of Employment Relations
Internships Offered: Both
Average Number Per Year: 4
Departments: Newsroom
Applications Received: 30-60
Period of Availability: Summer
Duration: 8-10 weeks
Qualifications: College sophomores—seniors or graduates.
Application Procedure: Send cover letter/resume to contact.
Application Deadline: January 1

THE WORLD

See listing for Newspaper Printing Corporation

YORKVILLE INQUIRER

See listing for the News and Observer Publishing Co.

ZEBULON RECORD

See listing for the News and Observer Publishing Co.

Section 2

Internships In Magazine Publishing

5

The Business Press: Where The Jobs Are

Donald McAllister, Jr.—Chairman
Geyer-McAllister Publications, Inc.

Do the graduates of the top journalism schools know of a "secret" job opportunity that you don't?

They might. Guess where the largest single group of graduates from Northwestern University's Medill Journalism School graduate-level magazine publishing program are working?

If you guessed the big, well-known consumer magazines, newspapers, or even public relations, you're wrong. When graduates' careers were studied during an eight-year (1980 to 1988) period, *more than 20% of them worked for specialized business and association magazines,* compared to 14% and 12% for the next two highest classifications.

Admittedly, it wasn't always this way. If my family hadn't been in this business, I really wouldn't have known about the existence of trade magazines when I attended Medill nearly twenty years ago. About the closest we ever got to the business press was an occasional mention of special-interest consumer magazines.

Things are very different today. Now a number of the magazine prototypes created in Medill's program are specialized business titles, ideas like *Renovation Architect, Fitness Business,* and *Contract Health Care.* (The last title, targeted to alternative delivery system decision makers, was so good that it was purchased by a publisher.)

Our media has gained such acceptance at Medill that a top manager from a trade publisher spends a week on campus every year working with these students to create a new magazine.

Medill is not alone in giving attention to this important media. Approximately thirteen other journalism schools presently have regular full courses, five established in the last year alone. Another half dozen journalism schools devote at least one class session in their magazine courses to the specialized business press.

So Just What Is The Business Press?

Okay, you say, all of this sounds pretty good, but I still don't have much of an idea what these publications really are.

So let's start with a definition of specialized business publications or trade magazines *(also* sometimes called business papers or technical journals). Don't let the word "business" throw you off—we're not talking about general business publications such as *Business Week, Fortune* or *Forbes.* Business or trade magazines serve a specific field or function in business, industry, or the professions.

Whatever business someone is in or cares about—chemicals, banking, metal working, mining, construction, shipping and travel, etc.—and whatever the specific area in which they function —purchasing, design engineering, plant maintenance, sales, etc.—there is at least one business publication (and probably more) directed solely at their little corner of the world.

In fact, there are over 4,000 such publications, earning over $3 billion in revenue, and employing more that 100,000 people, devoted to nearly 200 distinct classifications of industry. Yet they are invisible to many people since, for the most part, they are not seen on newsstands or available in libraries.

And there are sub-groups, ensuring that every industry, every specialization, every *sub*-specialization, is covered by one or more magazines.

How important are these publications? The fact that they attract over 70 million readers annually and nearly 2 million advertising pages says they are very important indeed!

The largest *number* of trade titles (according to *SRDS*, which lists virtually every business publication in the U. S.)— over 350—are in the medical and surgical field, followed by metropolitan, state, regional business titles (nearly 150) and those devoted to some facet of the computer industry (about 115).

However, when it comes to revenue, computer publications are unquestionably #1, with over 65,000 ad pages, representing $600+ million annually. Electronic engineering titles come in second, with nearly 50,000 ad pages ($250+ million); restaurant/food service titles are third, with nearly 20,000 ad pages ($140 million).

What's Different About The Business Press

An editor on a trade magazine will be doing more things in a shorter period of time than at any other media. Basically, since these are smaller magazines, the junior editor isn't as apt to be pigeon-holed and, in fact, is *encouraged* to wear different hats in a short period of time.

Yes, you'll be doing your fair share of new product releases. But quicker than you think, you'll be editing, working in production, writing articles, covering shows, etc. The key thing is that you will be able to become an expert in a particular field.

In fact, trade magazine editors are, in many cases, *the* experts in a vast range of fields. This is particularly illustrated when the consumer press needs more information on a particular business topic—they always seem to rely on trade magazines!

A good example of this is *Milling and Baking News*, a 5,500 circulation trade publication for chief executives of milling or baking companies, which broke the story of the Soviet Union's purchase of American grain a few years ago. For weeks, Walter Cronkite, The New York *Times,* and the rest of the popular media relied on this publication for virtually *all* of their information on this major story.

Obviously, this magazine's influence (and that of many other trade publications) derives not from *how many* people read it, but *who* those people are. That's a major reason why advertisers don't mind paying a premium to reach the decision makers in a particular field, as much as fifteen or even twenty times the CPM (cost per thousand) of a major consumer magazine. They're willing to pay more to reach the *right* people, not simply *more* people.

Misconceptions You May Think Are Truths

Let's clear up some other misconceptions of trade magazines. Years ago, a definite segment of the business press were considered pretty shabby looking. But today, most of our magazines match the better consumer publications in color, graphics, and layout.

As with better consumer magazines, most trade titles keep advertising and editorial separate. A few years ago, one of our company's own publications won an award for criticizing industry manufacturers by name, which included several of our top advertisers, for announcing new products in advance of when they were actually available to the marketplace.

Don't be put off by the focused nature of the subject matter in trade magazines and think that we're looking for industry experts. We're looking for good communicators—just like any other media. With the possible exception of the most highly technical or scientific publications, the industry knowledge you need can be picked up along the way.

My advice: Seek out a specialized business publication related to an interest of yours. At a magazine job fair, I met a student who had worked with railroad operations for ten years. When he decided to switch his career to journalism, I introduced him to the editor of a railroad trade magazine, who hired him on the spot. They are both delighted with their decisions.

Emphasizing the fact that most of our media's publications are not too technical, less than a quarter of the editors learned about the industry which their publications cover in a formal classroom setting. More typically, a superior informally taught them about the field, and they "learned as they earned."

Should You Switch To The Business Press?

Why switch or consider the business press?

There are at least twice as many trade magazines as consumer publications. It's obvious where the most jobs lie. These job opportunities may be in smaller publications than consumer magazines, but they are not small publications. In fact, we have nearly half the ad volume of consumer magazines.

Try living on some of the newspaper or broadcast paychecks! *Folio* magazine's annual editorial salaries survey shows compensation for trade editors at the senior, associate, and managing editor levels equal to or actually ahead of that of consumer magazines'.

Add the fact that we offer employees the greatest chance of participatory management and employee profit sharing *and* the quickest path to potential ownership.

Which should lead you to only one question:

Now How Do I Get A Job There?

One of the best ways to approach our media is through the Business Press Educational Foundation, founded by Harold W McGraw, Jr., Chairman Emeritus of McGraw Hill. Now an affiliate of the American Business Press, it will be conducting its sixth annual intern program in the summer of 1990. This program is the largest one of its kind for our media and will place 25 students nationally this summer. Previous interns seem to like what they have seen.

More than half of the interns from the program's first three years have gone on to full-time positions in the business press. The following comment by 1987 intern Cassimir Medford of Baruch College captures the feeling of many of these interns. "It would be difficult for me to exaggerate the importance of my Foundation internship. When I started my internship at *Information Week,* I had not made up my mind what area of journalism I wanted to pursue. The fact that I am now an assistant editor at the magazine demonstrates the effect this internship has had on my future. I am proud to say that I am now a card-carrying member of the business press."

Instead of filling the office coffee cups all summer, this select group of students has conducted research, done interviews, written articles, and had their work printed. All of this is not by accident. The Foundation asks a number journalism faculty advisors each year for recommendations of top students who would be interested in working as interns on a trade magazine. In the fall, the Foundation contacts trade magazine publishers who want to sign up for the summer intern program.If you are interested, contact Marc Leavitt, Executive Director, or Phyllis Reed, Manager of Placement and Education Services, for more information.

And the Foundation's affiliate, the American Business Press, publishes a monthly employment round-up where publishers looking for people, and persons looking for positions, run notices. A few companies run ads for trainees. Conversely, some recent graduates run ads seeking entry-level positions. Contact Phyllis Reed for more information at the same address and phone number as above.

Then come join us in the rapidly-expanding world of the business press!

DONALD McALLISTER, JR. has been active in promoting specialized business publications at the college level as vice-chairman of the Business Press Educational Foundation, Inc. and as a member of the Specialized Business Press Advisory Board at New York University's Gallatin Division. He also currently serves on the American Business Press's Board and is a former chairman and board member of the Association of Paid Circulation Publications.

Mr. McAllister graduated from Northwestern University's Medill School of Journalism with a master's degree in 1971, after which he started full-time work with Geyer-McAllister, the company founded by his great uncle, Andrew Geyer, in 1877. He worked as both an editor and salesman before assuming management positions.

6

Editorial Internships Are Gateways To Careers

Robert E. Kenyon, Jr., Executive Director
American Society of Magazine Editors

Internships are gateways to jobs on magazine editorial and business staffs. This is evident from the number of editorial interns in the Magazine Internship Program, sponsored by the American Society of Magazine Editors, who have gone on to entry-level jobs on magazines and elsewhere in journalism—about 325 out of a total of more than 960. *(For details on internships on the business side, see the next chapter.)*

Magazines occupy a unique position in the world of communication. On one side are the news media—newspapers and broadcast; on the other, the definitive material contained in books. News comes and goes in hours or minutes, while the definitive information may take years to compile.

Magazines fit snugly between these two extremes—contemporary and up-to-the-minute, yet authoritative, responsive to trends and developments and readily adaptable to changing cultures. They provide current information, ideas, even inspiration.

The response of magazines to new developments and trends is dramatized by the annual compilation of new magazine titles produced by Professor Samir Husni of the University of Mississippi. In his 1989 report, he listed 491 titles in 41 different special-interest categories, ranging from art and antiques to youth. The six categories with the largest number of new titles were sports; automotive; crafts, games, hobbies and models; dressmaking and needlework; home service and home; and music.

What Internships Do For Everyone

Magazine internships are gateways to jobs on magazine editorial staffs because they give college students a realistic, firsthand view of what is involved in the editing and publishing of magazines. At the same time, they give magazine editors the chance to evaluate possible future additions to their staffs and a summer's worth of work from well-qualified editorial assistants.

A few comments from former interns now working on magazine staffs indicate what an internship can do for young journalists:

"My experience has been a total one—I have learned as much personally as professionally;"

"If I had sat down in early June and written down everything a 'perfect' internship would have entailed, the list would not have covered all of the remarkable experiences I ended up having while I was here this summer.

"Overall, my internship was fantastic and more rewarding than I ever could have imagined.'"

Editors, too, have good things to say about internships:

"Our staff is most enthusiastic about the fresh ideas and viewpoints the interns bring to our summers, and editors readily pitch in, teaching, advising and explaining."

"I also think the internship program is a learning opportunity for editors. Either we were very fortunate or the screening process is excellent, but in either case it was very helpful for me to know that there are qualified, enthusiastic, already well-trained women 'out there.' The internship program offers an invaluable experience to aspiring editors."

The Tasks Interns Perform

Interns' duties and responsibilities vary according to the operation and requirements of each magazine. Generally, however, they do the things that entry-level assistant editors do, but under closer supervision and instruction.

These tasks include: handling reader mail; initial readings of unsolicited manuscripts; basic research on articles in preparation; checking the facts in completed articles; copy editing; proofreading; writing heads and captions; interviewing people who may be subjects of future articles; covering press conferences; and attending editorial planning meetings. Depending on the magazine and its field, the intern may do some writing, even gain a few bylines.

Some internship programs are careful to include basic educational seminars, usually weekly meetings and discussions with various executives of the publications.

Structured Vs. Volunteer Programs

A structured internship program is one in which the participating magazines arrange a well-planned schedule for their interns, giving them responsible work to do and, therefore, attempt to create a real learning experience. Such a program will pay the intern an agreed-upon stipend.

Interns who are fortunate to be in such a program will also have opportunities to visit the business departments and learn how circulation and advertising are sold, what the promotion and research people do and how the magazine is printed and distributed. Such a program will usually allow an intern to meet and visit with the chief editor and other important executives of the publishing company.

There are other so-called internships that are really volunteer jobs in which the "intern" is likely to do more menial tasks and receive little or no compensation. While such an intern is exposed to the operation of a magazine editorial staff, it is not the kind of learning experience a structured program offers. A prospective intern should inquire about the duties involved in a voluntary program before accepting it.

ASME Internships

The ASME Magazine Internship Program begins with a four-day orientation session during which interns review the essential facts about editing and publishing magazines. They hear from prominent editors on how and why they edit their magazines. Art directors discuss the importance of layout and design and how the editor and art director work together to create a visual presentation that will appeal to their readers. Business executives explain the functions of advertising, circulation, production, research and promotion. ASME Intern participants also meet and talk with alumni of the program.

How Do You Qualify?

What does an editor look for in a prospective intern? Interns come from two kinds of colleges and universities: schools and departments of journalism and general liberal arts schools (that offer few or no journalism courses).

A journalism major should have had basic skill courses in reporting, writing and editing, be deeply involved in campus journalism and have worked at least one summer somewhere in journalism.

Being "deeply involved" in campus journalism means more than writing an occasional article for the newspaper, magazine or yearbook; it should involve ongoing editorial responsibility. A student who was managing editor of a campus publication in his or her junior year and is heading for the chief editorship next year is an ideal candidate. Such responsible positions give the prospective intern much-desired hands-on experience and indicate that commitment to journalism that is the foundation of any successful internship.

Interns may also come from liberal arts colleges and universities. The only way for such students to qualify for a worthwhile internship is to have had a top position on the college newspaper or magazine, having worked his or her way up through the usual preparatory steps. In addition, at least two summers should have been spent in journalism—reporting, writing or editing for an established publication.

Both journalism majors and liberal arts students should have a firm foundation in literature, history, political science, economics, natural science, foreign languages and sociology. Given the concerns of our society today and the direction of our culture, a journalist who is not aware of the basic facts and trends in these fields is at a decided disadvantage. Individual colleges and universities may have their own requirements for a degree, but surely any self-respecting institution would welcome a student who manifests an interest in these areas.

Entry-Level Jobs In Editorial

An entry level job on a magazine editorial staff is usually called *editorial assistant*, sometimes *administrative assistant*. The starting salary will range from about $14,000—

$18,000 or more, depending on the magazine and its geographical location. As a new staff member, you should plan to stay in that job for one to three years and expect modest increases in salary periodically.

Your pace of advancement will depend largely on your abilities and willingness to work hard at whatever tasks are assigned and to volunteer for those beyond the daily routine. After this probationary period, during which you are paying your dues, as it were—the progression is to *assistant editor, associate editor, senior editor, managing* or *executive editor* and eventually, if all goes well, to *editor* (or *editor in chief* or *editorial director*). As you advance up the masthead, your salary will keep pace, moving into the 20s and 30s, reaching finally into the high five figures or, in some cases, even six figures.

And How They Differ From Internships

Interns who get a full-time, entry-level job should realize that it is going to be quite different from their internship experience.

As interns, they were given special treatment—a form of tender loving care—shown how the various departments of the magazine worked together, had lunches or dinners with various staff members, even sat in on editorial meetings.

As staff members, they will be restricted to more routine tasks until they have begun the move up the masthead. There is a certain glamour and freedom in being an intern; neither carries over to a staff job. The rewards are there, but they have to be earned.

One last important note: New York City is the location of more magazine editorial offices than any other city in the country. So somewhere in your magazine career, New York is likely to play a part; but it probably shouldn't be at the beginning. Better to start your career somewhere else in the country.

There is an excellent list of publishers nationwide who offer intern programs in chapter 8. Use it.

ROBERT E. KENYON, JR. was the founding secretary of ASME in 1963 and instrumental in the establishment of its intern program in 1967. After serving a five-year term as president of the Magazine Publishers Association, he became its executive vice president in 1961, retiring from that position in 1974. Prior to joining MPA, he was publisher of *Printers' Ink.* From 1974 to 1978, when he returned to ASME as its executive director, he lectured and taught magazine journalism at a dozen schools of journalism around the country, including a stint as visiting professor and assistant dean at Northwestern University's Medill School of Journalism.

Mr. Kenyon received in 1989 a special National Magazine Award for "personal and professional excellence;" was named to the Publishing Hall of Fame in 1985 and was given an award for "outstanding service to magazine journalism education" by the Association for Education in Journalism in 1980.

7

Magazine Internships On The Business Side

**Bill Winkelman, Former Manager of Special Projects
Magazine Publishers Association**

Because magazines are so often viewed as strictly editorial products, many people don't consider magazine publishing to be a business. It is. In some respects, it's much like any other business: publishers are trying to sell their products (the magazines) to customers.

But the business of magazine publishing is fairly unique, in that publishers are selling two distinct products to two different kinds of customers—the magazine itself to its readers, the readers to its advertisers.

The business side of magazines is definitely more mysterious than the editorial side. The difficulty of learning about it is compounded by the fact that very few schools offer courses in magazine publishing.

So internships are especially valuable in gaining an understanding of "publishing." Business internships are generally found in either the Advertising or Circulation departments, supporting one of the two primary business activities—selling space in the magazine to advertisers or selling the magazine to consumers.

Important skills to bring to an internship and to put on your resume include computer literacy, useful in many internships, but especially so in more quantitative areas such as circulation planning and analysis. People skills are very important, especially on the advertising sales side, where developing and maintaining relationships is crucial.

Finding An Internship

If you are looking for an internship in magazine publishing, you must first become familiar with the business. Start by reading the many articles by top professionals on virtually every specialization that are included in the *Magazines Career Directory,* also published by the Career Press, which should be in your library. Then study other sources—especially *Folio* magazine, the trade magazine of the magazine industry, which also publishes several excellent books.

Most major magazine publishers are headquartered in New York City, but one can find magazine publishers in almost every region of the country—other major centers for publishing are Chicago, Los Angeles, Boston and Philadelphia. Wherever there are consumers, magazines are sure to follow. Your best chance for a paid internship will be at a large publication.

Learning About Individual Publishers

Getting an internship requires hard work. Prepare thoroughly by researching the companies you are interested in working for. The best source of information may be the magazines themselves. Most magazines have a "media kit" which they may supply to you (free of charge, if they do) if you request one. These kits are the promotional packages the magazines send out to advertisers; they'll tell you much about the magazine, how it's positioned, how it's sold, etc.

MPA Internships

The Magazine Publishers Association (MPA) sponsors an intern program in which students are placed with magazine publishers for the summer. What MPA looks for in applicants is what most publishers look for: a commitment to the print media, as evidenced by work on a publication—a school newspaper, high-school yearbook, college humor magazine, etc.— or volunteer work at a scholarly journal.

Also important is an interest in business as evidenced by summer internships, volunteer work, co-op positions, etc. Any such experience will distinguish you from the thousands of other people applying for summer internships in magazines. Entrepreneurial activities are especially attractive to many publishers, because they demonstrate your willingness to initiate and follow-through on projects and exposure to all the facets of running a business.

How to Apply

When you write to magazines for internships, try to individualize your letter. Since their medium is words, magazine people are especially sensitive to (i.e., dislike intensely) form letters. Write why you are interested in that particular magazine. Suggest what you would do if *you* were publisher, advertising director or circulation director. Don't shy away from creativity.

Although many publishers don't start looking for interns until a month or two before they plan to hire, you should start your search as early as possible. Utilize all your contacts— family, friends, professors, etc. It is difficult to get an internship, but a friendly phone call can take you a long way. Informational interviews are another good way to both learn about the industry and make contacts.

What You Should Expect
From An Internship

The most successful internships are generally those which are project-oriented. Make sure to ask what you will be doing and that you are not just a "gofer" hired because someone is taking a vacation. Although you can learn something about the business by just spending time in a publisher's office, nothing can replace hands-on experience.

Typical projects that interns have worked on include: creating and/or monitoring insert cards; developing a marketing plan for a new product or a special issue of the magazine; forecasting advertising demand for the magazine; analyzing advertising categories and suggesting ways in which the magazine could "break" new categories; analyzing magazine performance against industry averages; analyzing the profitability of various sources of subscriptions (TV, direct mail, insert cards), etc.

One of the most attractive aspects of a good internship is that it will make your full-time job search that much easier. Many publishers like to hire their interns back as full-timers the following year. You also will become familiar with the industry and its concerns and be able to put into words why you think you are a magazine person.

Among **BILL WINKELMAN**'s former responsibilities as manager of special projects at the Magazine Publishers of America was directing the MPA's Intern Programs for college juniors and MBAs. Before joining the MPA in 1984, he worked at Sonder Levitt Advertising in Philadelphia and Television Systems Marketing Co. in Horsham, PA. He is a graduate of the University of Pennsylvania and is currently an MBA candidate at the Wharton School.

8

Internship Listings: U.S. And Canada

The listings are pretty self-explanatory. Following the name, address and telephone number of the publisher or magazine, we listed three items of information about each:

The **Types** of magazines they publish (consumer, trade, professional journals, etc.);

A current list of those **Titles;**

And the **Total Employees** at the company. This will give you an excellent idea of the relative size of the magazine/publisher and the types of magazines you'd be working on.

The rest of the information in each listing relates specifically to the internships each company offers and are identicial to those in chapters 4 and 12. See chapter 4 for an explanation of each of these.

Before the listings begin, we've included a list of those magazines and publishers that do not offer internships, in the belief that this information is as essential as knowing about those who do. This list will eliminate many publishers you may have been targeting and make your search more effective.

Magazines That Do *Not* Offer Internships

(C) denotes a Canadian agency

Alberto's Fishing & Hunting
Magazine (C)
Angler & Hunter Magazine (C)
A/S/M Communications, Inc.
Barks Publications, Inc.
Billboard Publications, Inc.
Blue Stone News (C)
BMT Publications, Inc.
Canadian Money Saver (C)
Canadian Sportsman (C)
City Home Publishing, Inc.
City Published Reader's Digest (C)
Conde Nast Publications, Inc.
County Magazine (C)
Diamandis Communications
Family Communications Inc. (C)
Faulkner & Gray, Inc.
Forbes
Gallant/Charger Publications, Inc.
Hart Publications, Inc.
Hayden/VNU Publishing Company
Hearst Magazines Division
Heldrey Publications
H&W Publishing Limited (C)
Insight Publishing Ltd. (C)
Island Grower (C)
Johnson Publishing Company, Inc.
Kids Canada Publishing Corp. (C)
Knapp Communications Corp.
Lake Publishing Corporation
Legion Magazine (C)
Ludcum (C)

Maclean Hunter Media, Inc.
Maher Publications
McGraw Hill, Inc.
Meredith Corporation
Michigan Living Magazine
Murdoch Magazines
New York Times Co. Magazine
Group
Official Airline Guides, Inc.
Oildon Publishing Company of
Texas
Pacific Tribune (C)
Philadelphia Magazine
Playboy Enterprises, Inc.
Practical Communications, Inc.
Professional Publishing Assoc. (C)
Saturday Night (C)
Scott Periodicals Corp.
Scranton Gillette Communications
Selective Media (C)
Small Business (C)
Sounds & Visions (C)
Taunton Press
Telemedia Publishing (C)
13-30 Corporation
Time Magazine (C)
Transcontinental Publication
Wicklow Hills Publishing Co. Inc. (C)
Writers Life Line (C)

Magazine Internship Listings

AAA MICHIGAN
17000 Executive Plaza Drive
Dearborn, MI 48126
313-336-0509

Type Published: Consumer

Titles Published: Michigan Living, and five in-house publications.

Total Employees: 4,000+ in all branches

Internship Contact: Nancy Sarpolis, Publications

Internships Offered: Non-Salaried

Yearly Number Available: 4-5

Applications Received: 20-25

Period of Availability: Year-round

Duration: 10-12 weeks

Duties & Responsibilities: Lots of writing for the five internal newsletters plus filler-type articles for *Michigan Living*. Editing, proofreading and introduction to dummy layout and design. Some public relations, including press releases.

Qualifications: College juniors or seniors preferred.

Application Procedure: Send cover letter, resume and writing samples to contact.

Application Deadline: Flexible

AMERICAN BABY, INC
A subsidiary of Cahners Publishing
470 Park Avenue
New York, NY 10011
212-689-3600

Type Published: Consumer

Titles Published: American Baby, Childbirth Educator, First Year of Life, Childbirth '89

Total Employees: 47

Internship Contact: Judith Nolte, Editor

Internships Offered: Salaried

Yearly Number Available: 1

Departments: Editorial

Period of Availability: Summer

Duration: 2 months

Qualifications: College junior or senior preferred.

Application Procedure: Send cover letter and resume to contact or apply through American Society of Magazine Editors (see listing later in this chapter).

AMERICAN EXPRESS PUBLISHING CORP.
A division of American Express Travel Related Ser.
1120 Avenue of the Americas
New York, NY 10036
212-382-5600

Type Published: Consumer

Titles Published: Food & Wine, Travel & Leisure, New York Woman, LA Style

Total Employees: 200

Internship Contact: American Society of Magazine Editors (see separate listing)

Internships Offered: Salaried

Yearly Number Available: 3-5

Departments: Editorial, Circulation, Marketing & Sales

Period of Availability: Summer

Duration: 2-3 months

Duties & Responsibilities: "Interns aren't coddled; they do real work."

Qualifications: College juniors or seniors.

Application Procedure: Follow procedure detailed in listing for American Society of Magazine Editors.

Decision Date: May 21

AMERICAN MANAGEMENT ASSOCIATION
135 West 50th Street
New York, NY 10020
212-586-8100

Type Published: Professional Journals

Titles Published: Compensation & Benefits, Compflash, Foresight, Intrapreneurial Excellence, Management Review, Management Solutions, Managing New York State, Organizational Dynamics, Personnel, Supervisory Sense, Trainer's Workshop

Total Employees: 700

Internship Contact: George Harmon, Dir. of Human Resource Development

Internships Offered: Non-Salaried

Yearly Number Available: 10

Departments: All
Period of Availability: Flexible
Duration: 2 months
Application Procedure: Send cover letter/resume to contact.

AMERICAN SOCIETY OF MAGAZINE EDITORS
Magazine Center
575 Lexington Avenue
New York, NY 10022
212-752-0055

This is a key association in the magazine field, associated with the Magazine Publishers Association (see later listing). ASME's Internship program was established in 1967.

Internship Contact: Robert E. Kenyon, Jr., Executive Director

Internships Offered: Salaried ($250/wk). Interns are responsible for own travel expenses to New York City and for own housing expenses (though dormitory space, including meals, are often available at reduced cost by arrangement with ASME).

Yearly Number Available: 50

Departments: Editorial

Period of Availability: Summer

Duties & Responsibilities: Interns are assigned primarily to major magazines throughout the New York area (although in 1987, six interns were assigned to magazines in Washington, DC, one to *Sunset* in California and one to Whittle Communications in Tennessee).

The program includes the performance (under supervision) of such editorial tasks as handling reader mail, evaluating unsolicited manuscripts, researching articles, checking facts, writing leads and captions, proofreading, copy editing, interviewing, covering press conferences and attending editorial meetings. At some magazines, there will be writing opportunities, even a few by-lines. There will also be opportunities to see how other departments of the magazine function.

Qualifications: Students must be completing their junior year and returning to school the following Fall for a full senior year. Journalism majors should have taken some courses in reporting, writing and editing. It helps if they have worked on the campus magazine, newspaper or yearbook, preferably in a responsible editorial position. A previous summer job or internship in journalism is a plus. Liberal arts majors must have held responsible positions on the campus magazine, newspaper or yearbook and have had at least one summer job or internship somewhere in journalism. The cover letter is an important indication of experience, interest, attitudes and motivation. The letter from a dean, department head or professor (see below) who personally knows the student's journalistic abilities and experience is an important support document. Only one student per school is usually selected.

Application Procedure: Each application package must include the following elements:

1) The application form (available from ASME, but also mailed in October to deans, department heads and university offices requesting such information), signed by the student and by a dean or department head;

2) a letter from the student, expanding on the information in the application, especially activity or experience in campus journalism, internships or summer jobs in journalism, courses taken or planned, previous summer activity, extracurricular activity, magazines regularly read and, most importantly, why the student wants to be an intern, what is expected from the experience and what he or she hopes to contribute to the assigned magazine;

3) a supporting letter from a dean, department head or professor (see above);

4) if possible, a letter from a former intern indicating the student's qualifications;

5) a recent black & white portrait photograph, no smaller than 2 1/2" x 3 1/2" and no larger than 3 1/2" x 5 1/2". A passport photo will suffice;

6) Examples of the student's writing ability—e.g., tear sheets from the college magazine or newspaper—and of editing skills—e.g., edited proofs or editing exercises;

7) a stamped, self-addressed postcard for notification of receipt of application material.

Applications which have glaring errors in grammar, spelling, punctuation, or syntax will not be considered. All material must be typewritten. Incomplete applications will not be considered.

Application Deadline: Applications must be postmarked by December 15.

Decision Date: March 1 (Notification of specific magazine assign.—April 15.)

ASPEN PUBLISHERS, INC.
A subsidiary of Wolters Samsom Group
1600 Research Blvd.
Rockville, MD 20850
301-251-5064

Type Published: Professional Journals

Titles Published: 29 specialized publications in Clinical Medicine, Special Education/Language, Allied Health

Total Employees: 300

Internship Contact: Sandy Robinson, Human Resources Manager

Internships Offered: Salaried

Yearly Number Available: 1-2

Departments: Accounting, Graphic Arts
Period of Availability: Flexible
Qualifications: College juniors or seniors preferred.
Application Procedure: Send cover letter/resume to contact.

ASSOCIATED BUSINESS PUBLICATIONS
41 East 42nd Street—Suite 921
New York, NY 10017
212-490-3999

Type Published: Trade
Titles Published: NASA Tech Briefs
Total Employees: 20
Internship Contact: Frank Nothaft, Executive Vice President; Anita Weissman, Circulation Director/Office Manager
Internships Offered: Salaried
Yearly Number Available: 1
Applications Received: 6
Period of Availability: Flexible
Duration: 2-3 months
Application Procedure: Send cover letter/resume to contact.
Decision Date: March 15

ASSOCIATION FOR EDUCATION IN JOURNALISM
NYU Summer Internship Program for Minorities
Institute of Afro-American Affairs
New York University
269 Mercer Street—Suite 601
New York, NY 10003
212-998-2130

Internship Contact: Sidique A. Wai, Program Coordinator
Internships Offered: Salaried ($200 minimum)
Average Number Per Year: 15-20
Departments: Newspapers, Magazines, Broadcasting
Applications Received: 100-200
Period of Availability: Summer
Duration: 10 weeks (35 hrs/wk)
Duties and Responsibilities: Once accepted into program, intern is placed with a participating company (e.g., New York Times, Ms. magazine, AT&T, etc.). Interns are also enrolled in a two-credit course, Journalism and Minorities. Workshops and panels available.

Qualifications: Must be a minority; full-time college junior or senior with top academic standing. Educational interests in journalism.

Application Procedure: Send cover letter, resume, transcript, faculty recommendations (2) and application. Those wishing to participate in a broadcasting internship must submit TV/Audio cassette.

Application Deadline: Dec. 3 for letter of request; Dec. 17 for application.

ATLANTA ART PAPERS, INC.
Box 77348
Atlanta, GA 30357
404-588-1837

Type Published: Consumer
Titles Published: Art Papers
Total Employees: 5
Internship Contact: Editor
Internships Offered: Non-Salaried (credit, if school agrees)
Yearly Number Available: 2-4
Departments: Editorial, Design
Applications Received: 20-25
Period of Availability: Year-round
Duration: 1-2 months
Duties & Responsibilities: Projects, minimal clerical duties.
Qualifications: Editorial—College junior or senior; writing and word processing skills. Art—College junior or senior; art history major or courses preferred; art experience.
Application Procedure: Send cover letter/resume to contact.

ATLANTIC CITY MAGAZINE
1637 Atlantic Avenue
Atlantic City, NJ 08401
609-348-6886

Type Published: Consumer (monthly city magazine)
Titles Published: Atlantic City Magazine
Total Employees: 18
Internship Contact: Office Manager
Internships Offered: Non-Salaried (credit may be arranged)
Yearly Number Available: 2-3
Departments: Editorial
Applications Received: 12-18
Period of Availability: Year-round

Duration: 2-3 months

Duties & Responsibilities: Research, writing, editorial production art and basic work throughout department. Work on editorial index—intern's input and ideas welcomed.

Qualifications: College juniors or seniors; writing background and demonstrable skills. If from local area, interview required.

Application Procedure: Call or send cover letter/resume to contact.

BAM PUBLICATIONS
5951 Canning Street
Oakland, CA 94609
415-652-3810

Type Published: Consumer

Titles Published: Bam Magazine, Microtimes

Total Employees: 60

Internship Contact: Erica Stein

Internships Offered: Both

Yearly Number Available: 1

Departments: Editorial

Period of Availability: Summer

Duration: 2-3 months

Application Procedure: Send cover letter/resume to contact.

BEST-MET PUBLISHING COMPANY
5537 Twin Knolls Road—Suite 438
Columbia, MD 21045
301-730-5013

Type Published: Trade

Titles Published: Mid-Atlantic Food Service News, Food World, Food Trade News

Total Employees: 10

Internship Contact: Laura Lang, Office Manager

Internships Offered: Salaried

Yearly Number Available: 2

Departments: Editorial

Applications Received: 12

Period of Availability: Flexible

Duration: 2-6 months

Duties & Responsibilities: Writing copy, working on feature stories, proofreading.

Qualifications: College juniors or seniors.

Application Procedure: Send cover letter/resume to contact.

BILL COMMUNICATIONS
633 Third Avenue
New York, NY 10017
212-986-4800

Type Published: Trade

Titles Published: Incentive Marketing, Institutional Distribution, Jobber Retailer, Sales & Marketing Management, Modern Tire Dealer, Restaurant Business, Successful Meetings, Plastics Technology, Restaurant and Hotel Design, Long Term Contemporary Care, RX: Homecare Incentive

Total Employees: 290

Internship Contact: Irene Ricalde

Internships Offered: Salaried

Yearly Number Available: 3

Departments: Editorial

Period of Availability: Summer

Duration: 8-10 weeks

Duties & Responsibilities: Proofreading, some writing.

Qualifications: College juniors or seniors.

Application Procedure: Send cover letter/resume to contact.

BOSTON MAGAZINE
300 Massachusetts Avenue
Boston, MA 02115
617-262-9700

Type Published: Consumer

Titles Published: Boston Magazine

Total Employees: 50

Internship Contact: Alana Connolly

Internships Offered: Non-Salaried

Yearly Number Available: 12 per semester

Departments: Editorial, Promotion, Advertising, Advertising Sales, Art

Applications Received: 40-60

Period of Availability: Summer, Spring, Fall

Duration: One semester (2-3 days/wk)

Duties & Responsibilities: Editorial—Work directly with writers; research, proofread, etc. Advertising—Provide basic support to two-person staff; write press releases. Advertising sales—Support sales staff; work on media kits; research. Promotion—Help with parties, etc.

Qualifications: College juniors and seniors.

Application Procedure: Send cover letter/resume to contact. Editorial interns should submit writing samples.

Application Deadline: At least two months before student wants to start.

CARSTENS PUBLICATIONS, INC.
P.O. Box 700
Newton, NJ 07860
201-383-3355

Type Published: Consumer (special interest)

Titles Published: Flying Models, Railfan & Railroad, Railroad Model Craftsman

Total Employees: 25

Internship Contact: Harold Carstens, Publisher

Internships Offered: Salaried

Yearly Number Available: 1

Departments: Editorial

Period of Availability: Summer

Duration: 2-3 months

Duties & Responsibilities: Prepare copy and advertising, proofread, etc.

Qualifications: College juniors or seniors.

Application Procedure: Send cover letter/resume to contact.

CENTER FOR COMMUNICATION, INC.
570 Lexington Avenue—21st Floor
New York, NY 10022
212-836-3050

The Center for Communication is a nonprofit corporation offering a number of seminars for students interested in communication careers.

Internship Contact: Susan Toothaker

Internships Offered: Salaried ($500 stipend)

Yearly Number Available: 5

Departments: Advertising, Public Relations, Journalism, Broadcasting

Applications Received: 15

Period of Availability: Summer, Fall, Spring

Duration: Summer, Semester

Duties & Responsibilities: Research seminar topics, collect clippings, call guests, compile annotated bibliography, attend seminars and work on all aspects of their production.

Qualifications: College or graduate students; must be interested in communications.

Application Procedure: Send cover letter/resume to contact.

CHILTON PUBLISHING COMPANY
Chilton Way
Radnor, PA 19089
215-964-4000

Type Published: Trade, Professional, Medical

Titles Published: Approximately 20, including Food Engineering, Iron Age, Jewelers' Circular Keystone and Hardware Age

Internship Contact: Marilyn McLaughlin

Internships Offered: Both

Yearly Number Available: 3-4

Period of Availability: Year-round

Duties & Responsibilities: Clerical duties are minimal. Company attempts to involve interns in writing and research so they make actual contributions to magazines. Interns are given high priority if they wish to apply for full-time employment after graduation.

Qualifications: College juniors or seniors preferred.

Application Procedure: Send cover letter/resume to contact.

CMP PUBLICATIONS, INC.
600 Community Drive
Manhasset, NY 11030
516-365-4600

Type Published: Trade, Technical

Titles Published: Business Travel News, Communications Week, Computer Resellers News, Computer Systems, Electronic Buyer News, Electronic Engineering Times, Health Week, Information Week, Manufacturer Week, Tour and Travel News, VLSI Systems Design

Total Employees: 750

Internship Contact: Frank Nardi, Manager, Public Relations

Internships Offered: Salaried

Yearly Number Available: 4

Departments: Editorial

Applications Received: 80

Period of Availability: Summer, Fall

Duration: 3 months

Duties & Responsibilities: Paste-up, editing, copy editing, light writing.

Qualifications: College juniors or seniors preferred

Application Procedure: Send cover letter/resume to contact.
Decision Date: May—Summer, Mid-September—Fall

COMMERCE PUBLISHING COMPANY
408 Olive Street
St Louis, MO 63102
314-421-5445

Type Published: Trade
Titles Published: American Agent and Broker, Club Management, Decor, Life Insurance Selling
Total Employees: 60
Internship Contact: James T. Poor, President
Internships Offered: Salaried
Yearly Number Available: 1
Departments: Editorial
Applications Received: 100
Period of Availability: Summer
Duration: 6-12 weeks
Qualifications: College juniors preferred.
Application Procedure: Send cover letter/resume to contact.
Decision Date: May

COMMUNICATION CHANNELS, INC.
6255 Barfield Road,
Atlanta, GA 30328
404-256-9800

Type Published: Business—Consumer & Trade
Titles Published: Adhesives Age, Air Cargo World, Airline Executive, American City and County, Art Material Trade News, Better Nutrition, Business Atlanta, Cashflow, Comuter Air, Container News, Design Graphics World, Elastometrics, Midwest Real Estate News, Modern Paint and Coatings, National Real Estate Investor, Pension World, Robotics World, Selling Direct, Shopping Center World, Southeast Real Estate News, Southwest Real Estate News, Swimming Pool Age, Today's Living, Trusts and Estates, World Wastes, New England Real Estate Directory, Fire Chief, Aquatics, Access Control, Design Management World, plus various annual directory editions, postcard decks and convention dailies.
Total Employees: 320
Internship Contact: Arthur Sweum, VP/Editorial Director
Internships Offered: Salaried
Yearly Number Available: 3

Departments: Editorial
Period of Availability: Summer
Duration: 3 months
Qualifications: College juniors or seniors preferred.
Application Procedure: Send cover letter/resume to contact.
Decision Date: April 1

COWLES MAGAZINES
P.O. Box 8200
Harrisburg, PA 17105
717-657-9555

Type Published: Consumer
Titles Published: American History Illustrated, British Heritage, Civil War Times Illustrated, Country Journal, Early American Life, Fly Fisherman, The Original New England Guide, The Original New England Guide
Total Employees: 95
Internship Contact: Ruth Karabcievschy, Personnel Manager
Internships Offered: Salaried
Yearly Number Available: ?
Departments: General Administration, Advertising, Editorial
Applications Received: 100
Period of Availability: Summer
Duration: 2-3 months
Qualifications: College juniors or seniors preferred.
Application Procedure: Send cover letter/resume to contact.
Decision Date: April 15

DAVIS PUBLICATIONS, INC.
380 Lexington Avenue
New York, NY 10017
212-557-9100

Type Published: Consumer
Titles Published: Alfred Hitchcock's Mystery Magazine, Analog Science Fiction/Science Fact, Architectural Designs, Ellery Queen's Mystery Magazine, Income Opportunities, Isaac Asimov's Science Fiction Magazine, Sylvia Porter's Personal Finance Magazine, Woodworker Projects & Techniques
Total Employees: 90
Internship Contact: Phyllis Cohen, Personnel Administrator
Internships Offered: Non-Salaried
Yearly Number Available: 4

Departments: Editorial
Applications Received: 10
Period of Availability: Summer
Duration: 3 months
Duties & Responsibilities: Proofreading, typing, helping wherever needed.
Qualifications: College juniors or seniors preferred.
Application Procedure: Send cover letter/resume to contact.
Decision Date: June 1

EDGELL COMMUNICATIONS
(formerly Harcourt Brace Jovanovich)
7500 Old Ask Blvd.,
Cleveland, OH 44130
216-243-8100

Type Published: Trade
Titles Published: Over 100 business publications in a variety of medical, scientific and professional areas.
Total Employees: 220 (Editorial only, at this address. Advertising and Production offices separate.)
Internship Contact: Sharon Feador, Personnel Manager (and through Business Press Educational Foundation)
Internships Offered: Salaried
Yearly Number Available: 2
Departments: Editorial, Personnel, Promotion
Applications Received: 25
Period of Availability: Summer
Duration: 10 weeks
Application Procedure: Send cover letter, resume and writing samples to contact.
Decision Date: March 15

F & W PUBLICATIONS, INC.
1507 Dana Ave.
Cincinnati, OH 45242
513-531-2222

Type Published: Consumer
Titles Published: The Artist's Magazine, Writer's Digest, Decorative Artist's Workbook, The How
Total Employees: 170
Internship Contact: Kathy Schneider, Personnel Manager
Internships Offered: Salaried

Yearly Number Available: 7
Departments: Editorial, Marketing and Promotion, Advertising, Art
Applications Received: 80
Period of Availability: Summer, Fall
Qualifications: Must be college junior or senior.
Application Deadline: January 15
Decision Date: March 1

GEYER-McALLISTER PUBLICATIONS, INC.
51 Madison Avenue
New York, NY 10010
212-689-4411

Type Published: Trade
Titles Published: Geyer's Office Dealer, Gifts and Decorative Accessories, Playthings, Shipping Digest
Total Employees: 100
Internship Contact: Business Press Educational Foundation; ASME (See Appendix and separate listings)
Internships Offered: Salaried
Yearly Number Available: 3
Period of Availability: Summer
Duration: 10 weeks
Duties & Responsibilities: Assigned to one magazine, interns perform a variety of tasks, from planning sessions to meetings with editors. Minimal clerical duties.
Qualifications: Journalism students.
Application Procedure: Apply through ASME or BPEF.

GORMAN PUBLISHING COMPANY
8750 West Bryn Mawr Avenue
Chicago, IL 60631
312-693-3200

Type Published: Trade
Titles Published: Alimentos Procesados, Bakery Production & Marketing, Dairy Foods, Foodservice Bakery, Grocery Marketing, In-Store Bakery, Prepared Foods
Total Employees: 150
Internship Contact: Sue Bauer
Internships Offered: Non-Salaried
Yearly Number Available: 3
Departments: Editorial

Period of Availability: Summer
Duties & Responsibilities: Research, data input, setting up interviews.
Qualifications: College junior, senior or graduate student.
Application Procedure: Send cover letter, resume, and writing samples.
Decision Date: May 15

GRALLA PUBLICATIONS
A subsidiary of United Newspapers
1515 Broadway
New York, NY 10036
212-869-1300

Type Published: Trade

Titles Published: Bank Systems & Equipment, Builder's Kitchens & Baths, Contract, Corporate Travel, Facilities Design & Management, Gift and Stationery Business, Health Care Systems, Impressions, Kitchen & Bath Business, Meeting News, Multi-Housing News, National Jeweler, Premium/ Incentive Business, Real Estate Times, Sew Business, Sporting Goods Business, Travel Agents Marketplace. Advisory Division: Contact Lens Forum, Ophthalmology Management, Optometric Management

Total Employees: 500+

Internship Contact: Personnel Department

Internships Offered: Salaried

Yearly Number Available: 4-5

Departments: Editorial

Opportunities: No information available.

HARCOURT BRACE JOVANOVICH PUBLICATIONS
See listing for Edgell Communications

HARPER'S MAGAZINE
2 Park Avenue
New York, NY 10016
212-614-6500

Type Published: Consumer
Titles Published: Harper's
Total Employees: 25
Internship Contact: Ilena Silverman
Internships Offered: Non-Salaried
Yearly Number Available: 10
Applications Received: 50
Period of Availability: Year-round

Duration: 3-5 months

Duties & Responsibilities: Interns are an intricate part of the process. All interns do fact checking for *Harper's Index*. They do general tasks, including research, corresponding with writers, finding documents, etc. *Harper's* has low employee turnover, but interns have a good chance of being hired after graduation if an opening develops.

Qualifications: College sophomores—seniors; recent graduates; career changers.

Application Procedure: Call and request an application from receptionist.

HOUSTON MAGAZINE
P.O. Box 25386
Houston, TX 77265
713-524-3000

Type Published: Consumer

Titles Published: Houston; Symphony program guide for Houston Symphony

Total Employees: 30

Internship Contact: Katherine Guild

Internships Offered: Salaried ($75/wk)

Yearly Number Available: 10-15

Departments: Editorial, Production

Applications Received: 60

Period of Availability: Summer, Spring, Fall

Duties & Responsibilities: Some clerical, fact checking, proofreading, writing, research.

Qualifications: Upper classmen preferred with strong English background. Should be able to write well and produce quickly. Must be flexible, enthusiastic and dependable. Must work 16 hours minimum per school year.

Application Procedure: Send resume, cover letter (expressing student's interests and why they want to be an intern), and samples showing creativity, grammar and proficiency in writing a lead. Personal interview will be necessary.

Application Deadline: Aug. 5—Summer; April 7—Spring; Nov. 3—Fall.

INTERNATIONAL THOMSON RETAIL PRESS
345 Park Avenue South
New York, NY 10010
212-686-7744

Type Published: Trade

Titles Published: Consumer Electronics, Consumer Electronics Show Daily, Video Business, Auto Sound and Communication, Toy & Hobby World,

Cablevision, Communication Engineering and Design, Non-Food Merchandise, Convenience Store Management, Modern Floor Covering Business
Total Employees: 155
Internship Contact: Personnel
Internships Offered: Salaried
Yearly Number Available: 1
Period of Availability: Summer
Duration: 2-3 months
Opportunities: NA

INTERTEC PUBLISHING CORP.
P.O. Box 12901
Overland Park, KS 66212
913-888-4664

Type Published: Trade
Total Employees: 325
Internship Contact: Personnel
Internships Offered: Salaried
Yearly Number Available: 1-5
Applications Received: 30
Period of Availability: Summer
Duration: 12 weeks

Qualifications: College juniors or seniors preferred. Company gives major preference to local colleges.
Application Procedure: Send cover letter/resume to contact.
Decision Date: April 15

KIWANIS INTERNATIONAL
3636 Woodview Trace
Indianapolis, IN 46268
317-875-8755

Type Published: Association
Titles Published: Kiwanis Magazine
Total Employees: 132
Internship Contact: Program through Ball State University.
Internships Offered: Salaried
Yearly Number Available: 4
Departments: Editorial
Period of Availability: Flexible
Opportunities: NA

LOS ANGELES MAGAZINE
1888 Century Park East
Los Angeles, CA 90067
213-557-7569

Type Published: Consumer

Titles Published: Los Angeles (monthly city magazine)

Total Employees: 40

Internship Contact: Personnel

Internships Offered: Non-Salaried

Yearly Number Available: 1-2

Departments: Editorial, Advertising

Applications Received: 15-30

Period of Availability: Summer

Duration: 12 weeks

Qualifications: College juniors.

Application Procedure: Send cover letter/resume to contact.

MAGAZINE PUBLISHERS ASSOCIATION
575 Lexington Avenue
New York, NY 10022
212-752-0055

Undergraduate Program:

Internship Contact: Ms. Bonnie Lee

Internships Offered: Salaried ($300/wk). Interns pay own travel expenses and are responsible for room and board. Room and board in a local college dormitory may be available (approx. cost for summer $1,500).

Yearly Number Available: 25-30

Departments: Advertising Sales, Research, Circulation, Finance, Marketing, Promotion, Production

Applications Received: 200-250

Period of Availability: Summer

Duration: Early June to mid-August

Duties & Responsibilities: Interns are assigned to particular MPA-member magazines (by which they are paid), and duties vary greatly according to the particular magazine. In some cases, the internships will involve participation in the day-to-day operations of various departments of a magazine, with assignments in such areas as circulation, production, advertising, promotion, finance, etc. In the past, however, many interns have spent the summer on one or two major projects that involve work in several of these areas, exposing them to the entire publishing operation.

A series of seminars are held at MPA's offices, at which interns are able to meet and talk with leading magazine executives.

MPA helps interns find jobs after graduation if they are interested.

Qualifications: Must be completing junior year of college and planning to return for senior year next Fall. A genuine interest in magazine publishing and a desire to participate as a full-time employee (though an intern) are essential to a successful internship.

Application Procedure: Application package should contain the following (submit all at once, if possible):

1) A completed and signed application form;

2) An essay (preferably typed; suggested length—2-4 pages), detailing any business experience, work or school experience in magazine or other types of publishing and communications; courses taken or planning; previous summer work activity; extracurricular activities; why the applicant wants to participate in the program, what is expected from the experience and what the applicant can contribute to a magazine;

3) An up-to-date resume;

4) One or two faculty or employer recommendations (optional, but useful).

Participating publishers make final intern selections. Interviews, probably in New York, may be required by some.

Application Deadline: As early as possible (before February).

Decision Date: March-April

MBA Intern Program:

Internship Contact: Ms. Bonnie Lee

Internships Offered: Salaried ($5,000 for 10-week summer program). Interns pay own travel expenses and are responsible for room and board. Room and board in a local college dormitory may be available (approx. cost for summer $1,500).

Yearly Number Available: 15-20

Departments: Advertising Sales, Circulation, Research, Development, Finance, Marketing, Production, Editorial

Applications Received: 200+

Period of Availability: Summer

Duration: Early June to mid-August

Duties & Responsibilities: The emphasis is on involvement. Interns are assigned to particular MPA-member magazines (by which they are paid), and duties vary greatly according to the particular magazine. In some cases, the internships will involve participation in the day-to-day operations of various departments of a magazine, with assignments in such areas as circulation, production, advertising, promotion, finance, etc. In the past, however, many interns have spent the summer on one or two major projects that involve work in several of these areas, exposing them to the entire publishing operation.

A series of seminars are held at MPA's offices, at which interns are able to meet and talk with leading magazine executives.

MPA helps interns find jobs after graduation if they are interested.

Qualifications: Students should have completed first year of business school (MBA program) and be returning for second year in Fall. (Students who started business school in January will generally be considered also.)

Application Procedure: Application package should contain the following (submit all at once, if possible):

1) A completed and signed application form;

2) An essay (preferably typed; suggested length—2-4 pages), detailing any business experience, work or school experience in magazine or other types of publishing and communications; courses taken or planning; previous summer work activity; extracurricular activities; why the applicant wants to participate in the program, what is expected from the experience and what the applicant can contribute to a magazine;

3) An up-to-date resume;

4) A letter from the dean or another appropriate official of the intern's school certifying that the student will have completed at least the first year (semester) of graduate business school by the June he/she wishes internship to start;

5) Up to three letters of recommendation (under separate cover, if necessary). Students may also submit samples of work, writing, etc.

Participating publishers make final intern selections. Interviews may be required by some, usually in March or April.

Application Deadline: Application postmarked by Feb. 16.

Decision Date: March-April

MEDIA AND METHODS MAGAZINE
1511 Walnut Street—Suite 1429
Philadelphia, PA 19102
215-563-3501

Type Published: Consumer

Titles Published: Media and Methods, Successful Woman in Business

Total Employees: 10

Internship Contact: Steve Clancey

Internships Offered: Non-Salaried

Yearly Number Available: 3-5

Departments: Editorial, Advertising, Graphic Design

Applications Received: 15-30

Period of Availability: Year-round

Duties & Responsibilities: Editorial—Writing, proofreading and checking laying, research, lots of fact checking. Graphic Design—Assist art director. Advertising—Assist in all aspects of sales, including making cold calls.

Qualifications: College juniors preferred; must have a strong interest in magazine publishing.

Application Procedure: Send cover letter, resume and clips (Editorial) or portfolio (Art) to contact. Interview required.

MOTHER JONES MAGAZINE
1663 Mission Street
San Francisco, CA 94103
415-558-8881

Type Published: Consumer

Titles Published: Mother Jones

Total Employees: 30

Internship Contact: Joanne Cabello

Internships Offered: Non-Salaried (stipend available for transportation costs)

Yearly Number Available: 6-8

Departments: Editorial, Research

Applications Received: 15+

Period of Availability: Year-round

Duration: 3 months or longer

Duties & Responsibilities: Editorial—Read unsolicited manuscripts. Research—Fact checking.

Qualifications: No restrictions—open to students, career changers, returnees to the work force, etc.

Application Procedure: Send letter, resume and clips to contact.

Application Deadline: Continually looking for good interns.

THE NATION INSTITUTE
72 Fifth Avenue
New York, NY 10011
212-242-8400

Type Published: Consumer

Titles Published: The Nation

Total Employees: 50

Internship Contact: Vania Del Borgo

Internships Offered: Non-Salaried ($75 stipend)

Yearly Number Available: 24 (8 people 3 times per year)

Departments: All

Applications Received: 100

Period of Availability: Year-round

Duration: 3-4 months

Duties & Responsibilities: *The Nation* is U.S.'s oldest newsweekly. It is a journal of progressive opinion with a focus on foreign policy and civil liberties. Interns do many duties, including fact checking and all kinds of research. Various departments offer specific other opportunities: Editorial—Evaluating manuscripts, proofreading. Business/Circulation—Assist in fund raising; etc.

Qualifications: Recent college graduates or those close to graduation—any major.

Application Procedure: Send the following to contact: Cover letter outlining interests; resume; two writing samples (which may or may not have been published); and two letters of recommendation.

Application Deadline: Three months prior to starting date.

NATION'S BUSINESS MAGAZINE
A division of the U.S. Chamber of Commerce
1615 H Street
Washington, DC 20062
202-463-5731

Type Published: Consumer

Titles Published: Nation's Business

Total Employees: 100

Internship Contact: Ms. Tia Plunket

Internships Offered: Non-Salaried

Yearly Number Available: 75 (majority in summer)

Departments: All (including TV studio, Media Relations, Personnel, etc.)

Applications Received: 200

Period of Availability: Year-round

Duration: One semester

Duties & Responsibilities: Two interns in photography and two in art per semester. None in editorial. Other opportunities in various departments. Duties vary greatly from department to department. Interns are given preference in hiring after graduation.

Qualifications: College students, any major.

Application Procedure: Send cover letter (detailing areas of interest, date of graduation and availability) and resume.

NETWORK PUBLISHING CORPORATION
254 West 31st Street
New York, NY 10001
212-947-6300

Type Published: Consumer

Titles Published: Soap Opera Digest

Total Employees: 30

Internship Contact: Lynn Davey, Managing Editor

Internships Offered: Both

Yearly Number Available: 1

Departments: Editorial, Art

Applications Received: 6

Period of Availability: Summer

Duties & Responsibilities: Filing, opening reader mail, dummying magazine.

Qualifications: College juniors or seniors preferred.

Application Procedure: Send cover letter/resume to contact.

THE NEW REPUBLIC
1220 19th Street NW
Washington, DC 20036
202-331-7494

Type Published: Consumer

Titles Published: The New Republic

Total Employees: 50

Internship Contact: June Haley

Internships Offered: Salaried ($200/wk)

Yearly Number Available: 4

Applications Received: 50+

Period of Availability: Year-round

Duration: Summer; September—May

Qualifications: College juniors or seniors preferred; previous journalism experience or other internships helpful but not necessary.

Application Procedure: Send cover letter, resume, two letters of recommendation and writing samples to company, Attention: Internships

Application Deadline: Summer—February 1; School year—May 1.

NEWSWEEK
444 Madison Avenue
New York, NY 10022
212-350-4415

Type Published: Consumer

Titles Published: Newsweek

Internship Contact: Annabel Bentley, Chief of Research

Internships Offered: Salaried (approx. $360)

Yearly Number Available: 4

Departments: Editorial

Applications Received: 400

Period of Availability: Summer

Duration: 12-13 weeks

Duties & Responsibilities: Work as reporter researchers—two in New York, two in a domestic Newsweek bureau (to be decided upon by Ms. Bentley).

Qualifications: Junior in college (at least); previous journalism experience, other internships and college newspaper experience are all important factors.

Application Procedure: Send cover letter, resume and writing samples to contact.

Application Deadline: December 15

Decision Date: Mid-February

NORTH AMERICAN PUBLISHING
401 North Broad
Philadelphia, PA 19108
215-238-5300

Type Published: Consumer, Trade

Titles Published: American School & University Magazine, Business Forms and Systems, Custom House Guide, Dealerscope Merchandising, The Designer, Forms Professional, Global Trade, In-Plant Reproductions, Magazine & Bookseller, Official Export Guide, Package Printing, Printing Impressions and Electronics, Publishing Technology, Sailing World, Target Marketing

Total Employees: 250

Internship Contact: Patricia Immis

Internships Offered: Both

Yearly Number Available: 1-5

Departments: Editorial Research, Art Production

Applications Received: 50

Period of Availability: Year-round

Duties & Responsibilities: Assisting regular employees in departments. No story writing. College credit not arranged.

Qualifications: College students. Some knowledge of personal computers helpful; some experience in field (college newspaper, previous internship, knowledge of magazines and their fields, etc.) helpful.

Application Procedure: Send cover letter and resume to specific department head. Interview may be required.

OUR TIMES
390 Dufferin Street
Toronto, ON M6K 2A3
416-531-5762

Type Published: Independent Canadian Labor

Titles Published: Our Times

Total Employees: 12

Internship Contact: Lorraine Endicott, Office Manager

Internships Offered: Non-Salaried

Yearly Number Available: 1

Period of Availability: Year-round

Duration: One semester

Qualifications: College student.

Application Procedure: Call for an application.

Application Deadline: Ongoing

PENTON/IPC
1111 Chester Avenue
Cleveland, OH 44114
216-696-7000

Type Published: Trade

Titles Published: Approximately 30 titles in the engineering, computer, equipment/office and restaurant fields.

Total Employees: 2,000

Internship Contact: Amy Bower

Internships Offered: Non-Salaried

Yearly Number Available: 2-3

Applications Received: 15-25

Period of Availability: Summer

Duration: 8 weeks

Qualifications: College juniors or seniors preferred.

Application Procedure: Send cover letter/resume to contact.

PITTSBURGH MAGAZINE
4802 Fifth Avenue
Pittsburgh, PA 15213
412-622-1360

Type Published: Consumer (monthly city magazine)

Titles Published: Pittsburgh Magazine

Total Employees: 21

Internship Contact: Rene Seavy, Administrative Manager

Internships Offered: Non-Salaried

Yearly Number Available: 9-15 (3-5 per semester)

Departments: Editorial, Advertising

Applications Received: 30-40

Period of Availability: Year-round

Duration: One semester

Duties & Responsibilities: Editorial—Research, fact checking, not too much writing. Advertising—Everything to do with the sale of ads.

Qualifications: College juniors or seniors.

Application Procedure: Send cover letter, resume, and editorial clips (if applicable) to contact.

Application Deadline: One month before intern wants to start (summer spots fill quickly; apply early for increased possibility).

PRIME NATIONAL PUBLISHING CORP.
470 Boston Post Road
Weston, MA 02193
617-899-2702

Type Published: Consumer, Trade, Professional Journals, Medical

Titles Published: American Journal of Alzheimer's Care, American Journal of Hospice Care, Health Care Recruiter, Nursingworld Journal, P.T.O.T. Job News, Sports High, Lab Tech./Med Tech.

Total Employees: 25

Internship Contact: William Haslam, General Manager

Internships Offered: Salaried

Yearly Number Available: 1

Departments: Editorial, Marketing

Applications Received: 10

Period of Availability: Year-round

Duration: 4 months

Qualifications: College juniors or seniors preferred.

Application Procedure: Send cover letter/resume to contact.

RACQUET MAGAZINE
32 West 39th Street—Room 204
New York, NY 10018
212-463-7760

Type Published: Consumer
Titles Published: Racquet magazine
Total Employees: 11
Internship Contact: Judith King, Editor
Internships Offered: Both
Yearly Number Available: 1 year-round; 4 each summer
Applications Received: 10-15
Period of Availability: Year-round
Duration: 12 weeks
Qualifications: College juniors or seniors preferred.
Application Procedure: Send cover letter/resume to contact.
Application Deadline: Ongoing

READER'S DIGEST ASSOCIATION, INC.
Reader's Digest Road
Pleasantville, NY 10570
914-241-5301

Type Published: Consumer
Titles Published: Reader's Digest, Family Handyman, Travel Holiday, New Choices
Total Employees: NA
Internship Contact: Naomi Morrow, Dir. of Training & Development
Internships Offered: Salaried
Yearly Number Available: 15-20
Departments: Editorial, Production, Marketing, Data Processing, Public Relations
Applications Received: 200
Period of Availability: Summer, school-year
Duration: Summer, one semester
Duties & Responsibilities: Differ depending on the recruiting department's needs.
Qualifications: Applicants should have backgrounds which demonstrate strong academic performance, excellent written and verbal communication skills and proven ability to think logically and analytically.
Application Procedure: Send cover letter and resume to contact.

REESE COMMUNICATIONS INC.
460 West 34th Street
New York, NY 10001
212-947-6500

Type Published: Consumer

Titles Published: Front Page Detective, Inside Detective, Master Detective, Official Detective, True Detective, Video Magazine, Video Magazine Specials

Total Employees: 40

Internship Contact: Jay Rosenfield, President

Internships Offered: Non-Salaried

Departments: Editorial

Yearly Number Available: 3-4

Applications Received: 15-30

Period of Availability: Summer

Duration: 8 weeks

Duties & Responsibilities: Special projects, as needed.

Qualifications: College juniors or seniors.

Application Procedure: Send cover letter/resume to contact.

Application Deadline: End of February

RODALE PRESS, INC.
33 East Minor Street
Emmaus, PA 18036
215-967-5171

Type Published: Health, Fitness, Sports, Gardening

Titles Published: Bicycling, Men's Health, Prevention, Rodale's Organic Gardening, Runner's World, Backpacker

Total Employees: 1,070

Internship Contact: Paul Ivankevich, Manager of Personnel Services

Internships Offered: Both

Yearly Number Available: 10-15

Departments: Magazine Editorial: On above publications. Other Editorial: Health books and newsletters; Health Research; Photography; Art. Business: Circulation/Marketing; Advertising promotion; Corporate Communications; Market research.

Applications Received: 100

Period of Availability: Summer

Duration: 8-10 weeks

Duties & Responsibilities: Project related; interns function like entry-level employees.

Qualifications: College juniors—especially if interested in returning to Rodale as full-time employees after graduation. Editorial—Journalism students or other students with experience with on-campus publications. Business departments (Circulation, Advertising, etc.)—Liberal arts students with quantitative skills and interest in a career in marketing. Limited internships for accounting and business students.

Application Procedure: Send cover letter, resume and writing samples (editorial only) to contact.

SAN DIEGO MAGAZINE
4260 West Point Loma Blvd.
San Diego, CA 92138
619-225-8953

Type Published: Consumer (monthly city magazine)

Titles Published: San Diego magazine

Total Employees: 35

Internship Contact: General Manager

Internships Offered: Non-Salaried

Yearly Number Available: 12 (3 at a time, 4 times per year)

Departments: Editorial, Art, Advertising

Applications Received: 30+

Period of Availability: Year-round

Duration: One semester

Duties & Responsibilities: Each department runs a separate internship program, so duties vary considerably.

Qualifications: College student (any year); no graduates.

Application Procedure: Cover letter, writing samples and resume to contact.

Application Deadline: Several months before intern wishes to start, especially for summer internships.

SCHOLASTIC INC.
730 Broadway
New York, NY 10021
212-505-3000

Type Published: Consumer, Educational

Titles Published: Home Office Computing, plus six professional magazines and 30 classroom magazines.

Total Employees: 1,300 nationwide

Internship Contact: Julius James, Human Resources

Internships Offered: Salaried

Yearly Number Available: 5-10

Departments: Editorial, Finance, Promotion, Marketing

Period of Availability: Summer

Duration: 10 weeks

Duties & Responsibilities: Interns are there to help out and learn. Approach is "meaty" and hands-on—for instance, interns in editorial will have something published before the end of the summer.

Qualifications: College juniors only.

Application Procedure: Call to request an application form.

Application Deadline: Late April

SCIENCE NEWS
1719 N Street NW
Washington, DC 20036
202-785-2255

Type Published: Consumer

Titles Published: Science News

Total Employees: 14

Internship Contact: Patrick Young, Editor-In-Chief

Internships Offered: Salaried

Yearly Number Available: 3-6

Departments: Editorial

Applications Received: 15-20

Period of Availability: Year-round

Duration: 3-4 months

Duties & Responsibilities: Act as staff reporters and writers.

Qualifications: Open to graduate students in science and journalism only.

Application Procedure: Send cover letter, resume and writing samples to contact.

THEATRE CRAFTS MAGAZINE
135 Fifth Avenue
New York, NY 10010
212-677-5997

Type Published: Trade

Titles Published: Theatre Crafts magazine, Lighting Dimensions, CUE International

Total Employees: 25

Internship Contact: Patricia MacKay, Editor and Publisher

Internships Offered: Modest stipends

Yearly Number Available: 3-5

Applications Received: 15-20

Departments: Art, Editorial, Circulation

Period of Availability: Year-round (One semester)

Duties & Responsibilities: Projects and varied clerical duties—secretarial, filing, opening mail...generally a "gofer."

Qualifications: Open to all levels of students, career changers, etc. Theater background a plus.

Application Procedure: Send cover letter/resume to contact.

TIME, INC.
1271 Avenue of the Americas,
New York, NY 10020
212-522-1212

Type Published: Consumer

Titles Published: Time, Life, Money, People, Fortune, Sports Illustrated, Southern Living, Progressive Farmer, Creative Ideas for Living, Southern Accents,

Total Employees: 35,000 nationwide (4,000 NY)

Internship Contact: Trish Rowland; Heather McGaughey—Finance internships for MBA students only.

Internships Offered: Salaried

Yearly Number Available: 30

Departments: Editorial, Circulation, Magazine Business

Applications Received: 250

Period of Availability: Summer (9 weeks)

Qualifications: College juniors or seniors preferred; MBA students for finance internships.

Application Procedure: Send cover letter and resume to contact; (editorial internships—through specific colleges only. Ask your college career office for details.)

Application Deadline: As early as possible

Decision Date: March 1

TIMES MIRROR MAGAZINES
380 Madison Avenue
New York, NY 10017
212-779-5000

Type Published: Consumer

Titles Published: Golf, Outdoor Life, Popular Science, Ski, Field & Stream, Home Mechanics, Yachting, Skiing.

Total Employees: 500

Internship Contact: Through ASME and/or MPA (see separate listings)

Internships Offered: Salaried

Yearly Number Available: 3

Period of Availability: Summer

Duration: 2 months

Duties & Responsibilities: Each department sets curriculum, but it is work, not merely clerical. Company wants to ensure each intern has a meaningful experience.

Qualifications, Application Procedure, Deadlines: See ASME and MPA listings.

VERNON PUBLICATIONS INC.
3000 Northup Way—Suite 200
Bellevue, WA 98004
206-827-9900

Type Published: Trade

Titles Published: Alaska Construction & Oil, The Nurse Practitioner, Pacific Banker, Pacific Builder, Seattle Business

Total Employees: 50

Internship Contact: Judy Vernon, Manager

Internships Offered: Both

Yearly Number Available: 1

Departments: Editorial

Period of Availability: Summer

Duration: 3-6 months

Duties & Responsibilities: Project mailings, work on directory listings, some editing.

Qualifications: College juniors or seniors.

Application Procedure: Send cover letter/resume to contact.

Decision Date: May 1

WASHINGTONIAN MAGAZINE
1828 L Street NW
Washington, DC 20036
202-296-3600

Titles Published: Washingtonian magazine

Total Employees: 100

Internship Contact: Katherine Dunbar, Asst. Editor

Internships Offered: Salaried (minimum wage)

Yearly Number Available: 8 (2 per semester)

Departments: Editorial

Applications Received: 125+

Period of Availability: Jan.—May, May-Aug., Sept.—Dec.

Duration: One semester

Duties & Responsibilities: Fact checking, proofreading, some writing, research.

Qualifications: College students (any year); interest in journalism. Some graduate students accepted.

Application Procedure: Cover letter, resume, and writing samples to contact.

Application Deadline: Nov. 15 (Spring); Feb. 15 (Summer); July 15 (Fall).

Decision Date: One month after application deadline.

WEIGHT WATCHERS MAGAZINE
360 Lexington Avenue—11th Floor
New York, NY 10017
212-370-0644

Type Published: Consumer

Titles Published: Weight Watchers Magazine, Fast And Easy Recipes

Total Employees: 30

Internship Contact: Mrs. Lee Haiken, Editor-in-Chief

Internships Offered: Non-Salaried

Yearly Number Available: 1-2

Departments: All

Applications Received: 25

Period of Availability: Summer

Duties & Responsibilities: One intern would "float" through sales, advertising, circulation and editorial. Another with interest in food would work in the magazine's test kitchens.

Qualifications: College juniors only.

Application Procedure: Send cover letter/resume to contact.

Application Deadline: As early as possible.

Decision Date: February

WHITTLE COMMUNICATIONS
505 Market Street
Knoxville, TN 37902
615-595-5400

Type Published: Consumer

Titles Published: 37, including American Dental Health Administrator, The Best of Business

Total Employees: 1,000

Internship Contact: Cindy, Recruiting

Internships Offered: Salaried ($175/wk).

Yearly Number Available: 30

Departments: Editorial, Art

Applications Received: 150

Period of Availability: Year-round (12 weeks)

Duties & Responsibilities: Similar to entry-level employees—interns work as editorial and art assistants. Will attend initial planning sessions and work closely on ideas for stories and execution (ways to depict them). Interns in both departments learn a lot about production. Art interns work on design and layout; editorial on research and writing, with a chance for by-line(s).

Qualifications: College juniors or seniors.

Application Procedure: Call or write contact for application form.

Application Deadline: Fall—June 10; Winter—Oct. 7; Spring—Dec. 9; Summer—Feb. 24.

WORKING WOMAN McCALL'S GROUP
230 Park Avenue
New York, NY 10169
212-551-9380

Type Published: Consumer

Titles Published: McCall's, Working Mother, Working Mother Digest, Working Woman, Cooking School, Beauty, Diet & Exercise Guide, Success

Internship Contact: Ethel Eisenheimer, Managing Editor

Internships Offered: Salaried (Summer $250/wk; Fall/Spring—credit only)

Yearly Number Available: 5-8

Departments: Editorial

Period of Availability: Summer, Fall, Spring

Duration: Two to three months (summer); One Semester (Fall, Spring)

Duties & Responsibilities: Interns spend about 40% of their time in Editorial, reading and reporting on unsolicited manuscripts, proofreading and performing clerical duties. The rest of the time they are rotated through other magazine departments.

Qualifications: Summer—Graduating seniors or graduate students; Fall/Spring—Juniors also accepted.

Application Procedure: Send cover letter/resume to contact. Interns are mailed a test to complete.

Application Deadline: Summer—Feb. 28 (test must be returned by March 31)

Decision Date: April 15

Section 3

Internships In Book Publishing

9

Careers In Book Publishing: Some Joys And Pitfalls

Nat Bodian, Marketing Consultant

One of the more pleasant aspects of a job in book publishing is that there is a thin line between work and play in many publishing positions. Because of this, many who earn their livelihoods in publishing find it difficult to leave the office behind and channel their creative energies in other directions at the end of the work day.

According to one psychotherapist, "publishing insiders report a difficulty in maintaining a clear distinction between work and leisure; many describe themselves as *always thinking about work*."

The reason, according to this psychotherapist, is that "people in publishing clearly enjoy each other on a number of levels. The shared passion for books and a mutual understanding of the intensity of the work has been the basis of personal relationships that extend beyond the job."

Joan Manley, former vice president for books at Time, Inc., put it this way: "The people who should stay in publishing are those who love it, despite gender...my only advice is to enjoy it to the hilt, and if you don't, get out. There's not that much money in it."

Let's Talk About The Money

A lot has changed in book publishing in the last two decades.

One major development that has contributed to increased interest in book publishing careers is the changing nature of the job environment. "Gender-specific" jobs, whether male or female, that existed in the 1960s have virtually disappeared, and salary differences have more or less equalized.

Another major deterrent to jobs in publishing in the 1960s and earlier has since largely disappeared. Despite the low salary levels for publishing jobs, especially entry-level ones, job applicants were expected to pay employment agency fees. By the mid-1980s, publishers, for the most part, were paying the fees themselves.

Perhaps most important of all, by the mid-1980s, publishing salaries in many job categories were nearly triple those 20 years earlier. A key reason why starting salaries in book publishing were traditionally low was the intense competition for starting jobs. This arose mostly from the romanticized attraction of the book industry for many young people just out of college.

As the late Curtis Benjamin, one-time chairman of McGraw-Hill, noted, "Every summer... eager graduates flock to New York and the few other major publishing centers, each yearning to become part of the glamorized literary scene. They beg for starting jobs at almost any wage. Naturally, this perennial supply of new recruits has a depressing effect on the wage scale."

What If You Get The Job?

Once involved in the publishing scene, many employed in or near the major publishing centers make an effort to involve themselves in the meetings, seminars, and luncheons of various publishing groups and expand their range of publishing acquaintances.

A primary reason is to share and exchange expertise with their peers. But there are two other compelling reasons. One is to build and enhance one's reputation as a publishing professional.

The second is that publishing career growth frequently requires a change of jobs—personnel turnover in many establishments is in excess of 30% a year. Taking advantage of such outside activities, many entry-level people can establish and maintain a network of contacts that can be useful in ferreting out or attracting other job opportunities.

Sometimes contacts in other publishing establishments will alert those they have met at meetings and seminars when openings are known to them or posted within their own organizations, even when they have given notice to a current employer.

Not all job changes result from intentional efforts or the results of personal networking, however. Many upgrade their publishing careers by responding to unexpected calls from executive recruiters or "headhunters," as they are more commonly known.

There are any number of such recruiters who take on search assignments for client publishing companies for specific job openings. These headhunters frequently telephone individuals at various publishing establishments looking for suitable candidates or for suggestions for names of individuals who might be called for the job assignment.

The author of this article, receiving such a call, was told by the executive recruiter that his name had been mentioned by individuals at three other publishing establishments called earlier. In turn, I supplied the name of someone I felt was qualified and whom I knew to be unhappy in his present position. He was called and subsequently accepted the position.

Not all individuals who engage in networking do so with a change of publishing jobs in mind. Occasionally, after building up a network of contacts (or upon retirement), some turn to freelancing or consulting and then utilize their contact network to continue in publishing as an independent.

Ready For Hard Work?

Not all jobs in publishing are fun and games, even in part. While the idea of a job in publishing has a glamorous ring, there are pitfalls in working in some types of publishing environments.

For example, there is less job satisfaction for those working in small, struggling houses which may be understaffed, have mediocre lists, and lack sufficient financial clout to properly promote them.

I recall one house I once worked for where part of my time —too much!—was devoted to making excuses to printers seeking payment of overdue invoices.

Coupled with this, however, is the fact that in smaller houses, there is usually much more chance for rapid upward advancement and more opportunities to participate in a broad spectrum of activities associated with the overall publishing process.

In larger houses, salaries may be higher, but your day-to-day functioning may be limited to one specific and possibly very narrow aspect of publishing. Further, a few large establishments have reputations for repressive environments, high turnover rates, and occasional mass firings. The reputation of a particular house often can be learned by talking to others in publishing. (Another reason to keep networking!)

With all of the joys and pitfalls of a job in publishing, the industry will continue to attract hopefuls—many of them the brightest of the bright—and to provide an unending source of challenging and stimulating careers for those who love the vibrant and exhilarating challenges involved in creating books.

NAT BODIAN is an independent publishing consultant residing in Cranford, NJ. Until mid-1988, he was, for twelve years, marketing head for various professional and reference product lines and encyclopedias at John Wiley & Sons. His 30 years of book marketing and book selling experience includes management positions for a number of leading scientific, technical and scholarly publishers, and, early in his publishing career, as head of sales for the Baker & Taylor Company.

He also enjoys an international reputation as author of seven book industry references including Bodian's Publishing Desk Reference, the classic two-volume Book Marketing Handbook: Tips and Techniques, The Publishers Direct Mail Handbook, and Copywriters Handbook: A Practical Guide for Advertising Promotion of Specialized and Scholarly Books and Journals. An eighth new publishing industry guide, The Book Word Thesaurus, was completed in 1990 and is now awaiting publication. He has been a speaker at numerous publishing group meetings and seminars and has written extensively for the publishing press both in the U.S. and the U.K.

Mr. Bodian is currently a contributing editor to the *SSP Letter of the Society for Scholarly Publishing,* and a monthly columnist for the *COSMEP Newsletter,* the publication of the International Association of Independent Publishers. He was a founder of the Professional Publishers Marketing Group and a 1986 nominee for the Publishing Hall of Fame.

10

Book Publishing In Canada: Career Opportunities North Of The Border

Les Petriw, VP, College, Professional/Trade Divisions
Copp Clark Pitman

In 1966, Morty Mint started his publishing career as a college sales representative for Collier Macmillan in Toronto. In the fall of 1989, after a six-year stint as president of Penguin Canada (with 184 employees and sales of $35 million), he was appointed President and CEO of Penguin Books USA, with a staff of 1,100 in New York and sales of $300 million.

In the early '70s, Anna Porter joined a Canadian publishing house known as McLelland and Stewart as an editor for its trade division. By 1987, she had not only founded a successful publishing firm—Key Porter—but also become chairman of Doubleday, Bantam, and the Literary Guild of Canada.

These two successful and fascinating individuals—our Canadian "superstars"—show how far hard work and ambition can take you in this business of publishing.

What *is* different about the publishing scene in Canada and the United States? Before I answer that, let me give you some facts and figures about the Canadian scene:

- Population as of 1988—(approx.) 26,000,000, of which 6,500,000 (approx.) are French-speaking.

- Toronto, Ontario has the highest concentration of publishing firms.
- More than 6,000 people are employed full-time in more than 225 publishing firms.
- The Canadian domestic book market (French and English) has an estimated value of $862.5 million.
- Books published in Canada account for 48% ($416 million) of the estimated market.
- A total of 45,038 Canadian books are in print.
- Trade books (general interest adult and children's books) make up 31% of Canadian-published book sales.
- Total sales of English-language publishing firms reached $555 million, of which $247 million came from the sale of imported books and 55% ($307 million) from the sale of indigenous books.
- Total sales of French-language publishing firms reached $143.6 million, of which 24% came from imported sales.

(Above information from 1986-1987 Statistics Canada, Culture Studies, Book Publishing in Canada, found in Canadian Book Publisher's Council booklet, page 17.)

Where To Get Trained In Canada

At present, there are three Canadian institutions that offer students excellent training for a career in publishing.

In the eastern part of Toronto, Centennial College offers a two-year program on Book and Magazine Publishing (approx. $400 per semester). This school would be of interest primarily to those of you wishing to work in the art or production departments, but there are some courses for aspiring editors and salespeople. For information, contact: Mr. Ron Dodge, Chairman, Centennial College, Warden Woods Campus, 651 Warden Avenue, Toronto, Ontario, M1K 5E9.

Over the past ten years, the Banff Publishing Workshop has produced a wonderful program for students interested in publishing. Every summer, twenty to thirty senior publishing executives go to the beautiful, scenic Rockies for a two-week period to teach and conduct seminars on all aspects of book publishing. Students not only listen to lectures, they partici-pate in engaging case studies, including the creation of a fic-titious publishing house and its editorial and marketing plans. The fee for 1990 is approximately $2,000 CDN. To receive more information about this workshop and its new spin-off, the Toronto Publishing Workshop, write to them at 696 Yonge Street, Suite 606, Toronto, Ontario, M4Y 2H7 or phone 416-924-1143.

Just recently, Simon Fraser University in Vancouver launched a one-year post-graduate book publishing degree program. To receive more information, contact Ann Cowan or Roland Lorimer (co-directors), Canadian Centre for Stud-ies in Publishing, Burnaby, BC or phone 604-291-3689.

And finally, Ryerson Poly-Technical Institute has started a part-time program (evening courses) for book publishing and by January 1990 will offer seventeen or eighteen half or full courses. Please contact Rosemary Shiston and Mary McDougall Mande at 350 Victoria Street, Toronto, Ontario, M5B 2K3 or phone 416-979-5000.

Where To Research
Canadian Houses

The most essential reference you need to locate all the key people already working in Canadian book publishing is The Book Trade in Canada (approx. $30), an annual publication available from Ampersand Communications Service Inc

(2776 Sheffield Road, Ottawa, Ontario, K1B 3V9, phone 613-749-9998). This book lists every publishing house in Canada, the names of the senior and middle managers, the number of employees, and the number of Canadian titles in print. Use this information in concert with the entry-level employment data contained in the *Book PublishingCareer Directory's* Job Opportunities Databank (see chapters 26 & 27 in the brand-new fourth edition) to target potential employers. (This book is also published by The Career Press and is an excellent introduction to the world of book publishing.)

I would suggest you not only mail your resume to the person in charge of hiring, but also contact that person by phone or in person. Most Canadian publishing houses are not large enough to warrant a separate personnel department, so this approach really is preferable. Since the industry in Canada is closely knit, most employers will help you and direct you to other firms looking for people.

Many U.S. and U. K. companies have subsidiaries in Canada. Getting started with one of these firms could eventually lead to international opportunities. For example, many people who started at McGraw-Hill Ryerson, a Canadian firm, have been transferred to Australia, the U.S., Africa, etc. Many of these multinational firms (as well as Canadian ones) are members of the Canadian Book Publishers Council. To obtain a complete listing of their names, write to this organization at 250 Merton Street, Suite 203, Toronto, Ontario, M4W 1B1, or phone 416-322-7011.

The Association of Canadian Publishers is an organization made up exclusively of Canadian-owned firms, many of which have produced exceptional internationally-renowned works as well as many regional and local titles. To receive more information, contact them at 260 King Street East, Toronto, Ontario, M5A 1K3, 416-361-8645. And don't overlook the Association of University Presses (59 Queens Park Cres., Toronto, Ontario, M5S 2C4, 416-926-7143). Both of these organizations are excellent sources of information for the aspiring Canadian publishing professional.

Newly-Emerging Opportunities North Of The Border

Finally, I wish to list a few positions that have emerged in Canada during the past decade due to the competitiveness of the market, positions which offer excellent opportunities, even for neophytes.

Literary agents have grown greatly in number and power in Canada. In the '70s, most Canadian subsidiaries usually received their parent house's "big books" routinely. However, just as the "free agent" concept radically changed baseball, big authors have become "hot commodities," too. Canadian publishing/distribution rights are now not automatically "given" to the parent's subsidiary; authors—and their newly-powerful agents—now expect to auction these rights to the highest bidder. Also, Canadian authors who write both fiction and non-fiction works are represented more and more by agents who auction their manuscripts both nationally and internationally. Thus, where there might have been only a couple of literary agents in Canada a decade ago, there are now many more. The Ampersand directory lists these agents.

Commission Trade Sales Reps existed a decade ago, but both their numbers and expertise have expanded significantly. And since many publishers cannot afford to have full-time reps out west or east, these groups have done very well. Of course, many of them had worked for other trade houses before going out on their own, but they have hired new associates directly from universities and bookstores. Again, these rep firms are listed in <u>The Book Trade in Canada</u>. If you feel you would like to be an entrepreneur and not confined to a corporation, this could be the job for you.

Special Sales has become an area of exciting and imaginative ideas. While most book selling still goes through traditional distribution channels (i.e., chains, independent bookstores, etc.), some companies, notably Penguin and Key

Porter, have found ways to sell their books to corporations and achieved significant reductions to the cost of their product. The all-time best selling special sale was masterminded by Mr. Norm Shiennan, Vice President at Penguin, who sold over *four million copies* of the Beatrix Potter books at 99 cents each through Shell gas stations across Canada. Contact medium to large trade houses to find out more about this growing area of opportunity.

Direct Mail has been an important marketing tool for legal publishers for years, but only in the last five years have other firms tried to sell their trade, medical, and professional books via mail order. While it is more expensive to mail in Canada than in the U.S., the advent of desktop publishing and microcomputers are allowing many more firms to take advantage of this method. I think the use of direct mail will grow significantly in the '90s, and firms will be on the lookout for bright people to fill positions such as copywriter and marketing coordinator.

Desktop Publishing is now being utilized more and more in publishing firms, and anyone with appropriate skills will find themselves in demand by houses planning to do their own typesetting. Many companies who have brought in these systems are on the "bleeding edge" of technology, as some like to say tongue in cheek. It has been hard work, with many frustrations and successes. Contact production and promotion department heads to explore opportunities in this area.

Any first job in publishing, be it a secretary, order desk clerk, sales rep, or copy editor, will allow you to see all the exciting "goings on" of the publishing house. No doubt, if you have great drive and ambition, you will probably end up as successful as Morty and Anna, who everyone in Canada acknowledges as our "superstars."

One final comment: If you wish to seek landed immigrant status, contact our Department of Immigration in Ottawa for all the rules and eligibility requirements.

LES PETRIW started his publishing career in 1978 as a college sales representative for McGraw-Hill Ryerson in Toronto, Ontario. In 1980, he was promoted to regional sales manager. He became general manager of the college division of Copp Clark Pitman in 1984. In subsequent years, he was made responsible for the professional, medical and trade divisions. In 1989, he was appointed vice president for those divisions.

Since Copp Clark Pitman represents eleven publishing firms from the U.S. and six firms in the U.K., Mr. Petriw travels extensively and has been able to observe the corporate cultures of many publishing houses.

11

Internship Listings: U.S. And Canada

The listings are pretty self-explanatory. Following the name, address and telephone number of the publisher, we listed three items of information about each:

The **Types** of publishing the house does;

Its total number of current **Titles in Print;**

And the **Total Employees** at the house This will give you an excellent idea of the relative size of the house and the types of books you'd be working on.

The rest of the information in each listing relates specifically to the internships each company offers and are identical to those in chapters 4 and 8. See chapter 4 for a complete explanation of each of these.

Before the listings begin, we've included a list of those publishers that do not offer internships, in the belief that this information is as essential as knowing about those who do. This list will eliminate many houses you may have been targeting and make your search more effective.

Book Publishers That Do *Not* Offer Internships

(C) denotes a Canadian agency

Academic Select (C)
Acta Press (C)
Addiction Research Foundation (C)
Ad-Lib Publications
Alfred A. Knopf, Inc.
Alfred Publishing
Alive Books (C)
Althouse Press (C)
Altitude Publishing Limited (C)
American Library Association
American Philosophical Society
Anglican Book Centre (C)
Annick Press Ltd. (C)
Aquila Communications Ltd. (C)
Arsenal Pulp Press Ltd. (C)
Aspen Publishing, Inc.
Atheneum Publishing
Aya Press (C)
Bantam Books, Inc.
Barron's Educational Series, Inc.
Ben Abraham Books (C)
Benben Publications (C)
Between The Lines (C)
Big Country Books, Inc. (C)
Birch Tree Group Ltd.
Black Moss (C)
Black Rose Books, Inc. (C)
Blizzard Publishing Ltd. (C)
Boston Mills Press (C)
Breakwater Books, Ltd. (C)
Bridge Publishing, Inc.
Broadview Press (C)
Brunner/Mazel Inc.
Brunswick Press (C)
Butterworth Publishers
Butterworths Canada (C)
Camden House Publishing (C)
Canada Law Book Inc. (C)

Canadian Arctic Resources Committee (C)
Canadian Council on Social Development (C)
Canadian Education Association
Canadian Energy Research Inst.
Canadian Inst of Resources Law
Canadian Institute of Strategic Studies
Canadian Library Association (C)
Canadian Museum of Civilization
Canadian Musical Heritage Society
Canadian Nuclear Association (C)
Canadian Plains Research Center
Canadian Red Cross Society
Canadian Scholars' Press Inc.
Canadian Stage & Arts Publications
Canadian Teacher's Federation
Canan Books (C)
Can.-Ed Media Ltd. (C)
Cannon Book Distribution Ltd. (C)
Carleton University Press Inc. (C)
Carolrhoda Books, Inc.
Carswell Publications (C)
Catholic University of America Press
Cavendish Books, Inc. (C)
CBC Enterprises (C)
CBS Educational & Professional Publishing
CCH Canadian Limited (C)
Centax Book & Distribution (C)
Centre for Resource Studies (C)
Charlton Press (C)
Children's Press
Coach House Press (C)
Coles Publishing (C)
Committee on Canadian Labour History (C)

Commoners Publishing Society (C)
Community for Legal Education (C)
Company's Coming Publishing (C)
Computofacts (C)
Contemporary Perspectives, Inc.
Copp Clark Pitman Ltd. (C)
Cormorant Books (C)
Coteau Books (C)
Crabtree Publishing Company (C)
Crossroad/Continuum
Cupress Limited (C)
David C. Cook Publishing (C)
Deneau Publishers & Company (C)
Detselig Enterprises Ltd. (C)
Dominie Press Limited (C)
Doubleday & Company, Inc. (C)
Douglas & McIntyre Ltd. (C)
Dundurn Press Limited (C)
Dushkin Publishing Group, Inc.
Encyclopedia Britannica
Everyday Publications Inc. (C)
Facts On File, Inc.
Facts On File, Inc. (C)
Franklin Watts of Canada (C)
Gage Educational Publishing Co. (C)
Garland Publishing
General Publishing Co. Ltd. (C)
Ginn and Company (C)
Grolier Educational Associates (C)
Grolier, Inc.
Grosvenor Books Canada (C)
GTE Discovery Publications, Inc.
Guernica Editions (C)
G.K. Hall & Company
Harcourt Brace Jovanovich (C)
Harlequin Enterprises Limited (C)
Harper & Collins Books Ltd. (C)
HarperCollins Inc.
D.C. Heath & Company
D.C. Heath Ltd. (C)
Henry Cuff Publications Ltd. (C)
Henry Holt & Company
Holt, Rinehart & Winston Ltd. (C)
Houghton Mifflin Company
Houghton Mifflin Ltd. (C)

Howard W. Sams & Company, Inc.
Human Sciences Press, Inc.
Hyperion Press Limited (C)
Iowa State University Press
Irwin Publishing (C)
John Wiley & Sons Limited (C)
Kluwer Academic Publishers
La Court Echelle (C)
Lerner Publications Company
Little, Brown & Co., Ltd. (C)
Longman, Inc.
Louisiana State University Press
McClelland and Stewart (C)
McDougal, Littell & Company
McGill-Queens University Press (C)
McGraw-Hill
McGraw-Hill Ryerson Limited (C)
Macmillan of Canada (C)
Mayfield Publishing Company
Meredith Corporation
Merriam-Webster Inc.
Merrill Publishing (C)
Merrill Publishing Company
Monarch Books of Canada (C)
C.V. Mosby Co. Ltd. (C)
Nelson (C)
Nelson Hall Publishers
W.W. Norton & Company, Inc.
Novalis (C)
NYU Press
Oberon Press (C)
Orca Book Publishers Ltd. (C)
Oryx Press
Oxford University Press (C)
Pantheon Books
Peguis Publishers Limited (C)
Pembroke Publishers Limited (C)
Penguin Books Canada Limited (C)
Pergamon Press
Peter Lang Publishing Inc.
Plenum Publishing
Prentice-Hall Canada, Inc. (C)
Rand McNally & Company
Random House, Inc. **(SEE P. 198)**
Random House of Canada (C)

Reader's Digest Association Ltd. (C)
Reid Publishing Ltd. (C)
Richard De Boo Publishers (C)
Samuel Weiser, Inc.
Saunders Book Company (C)
W.B. Saunders Co. Ltd. (C)
Scholastic-TAB Publications Ltd. (C)
Shambhala Publications, Inc.
Simon & Pierre Publishing Co. (C)
W. H. Smith Publishers, Inc.
South-Western Publishing Co.
Springer-Verlag New York, Inc.
St. Martin's Press
Stoddart Publishing Co. Limited (C)
Tab Books, Inc.
Thomas Allen & Son, Ltd. (C)
Time-Life Books, Inc.
Trans-Canada Press (C)
University of Chicago Press

University of Hawaii Press
University of New Mexico Press
University of North Carolina Press
University of Ottawa Press (C)
University of Toronto Press (C)
University of Washington Press
Univeristy Press of New England
University Press of Virginia
Van Nostrand Reinhold
Wadsworth, Inc.
Warren H. Green, Inc.
Weige Educational Publishers (C)
J. Weston Walch
Walker & Company
Warner Books, Inc.
Westview Press
Williams-Wallace Publishers Inc. (C)
Williams & Wilkins
World Book Childcraft of Canada.

Book Publishing Internship Listings

ABINGDON PRESS
201 Eighth Avenue
Nashville, TN 37200
615-749-6000

Types of Publishing: General, Religious

Titles in Print: 184

Total Employees: 1,200

Internship Contact: Vanessa Stewart, Employment Supervisor

Internships Offered: Non-Salaried (most)

Yearly Number Available: 2-3

Period of Availability: Year-round

Duration: 8-10 weeks

Qualifications: College students, any year.

Application Procedure: Send cover letter/resume to contact.

HARRY N. ABRAMS, INC.
A subsidiary of the Times Mirror Company
100 Fifth Avenue
New York, NY 10011
212-206-7715

Types of Publishing: Trade and art/illustrated
Titles in Print: 140
Total Employees: 150 (125 in U.S., 25 in Japan and Holland)
Internship Contact: Ellie Giannasco, Dir. of Personnel
Internships Offered: Both (Hourly pay—minimum wage)
Yearly Number Available: ?
Departments: Editorial, Public Relations, Art
Duties/Responsibilities: Primarily clerical. Interns do not work on projects.
Application Procedure: Send cover letter/resume to contact.

ACADIENSIS PRESS
Campus House
University of New Brunswick
Fredericton, NB E3B 5A3
506-453-4978

Types of Publishing: Books on Atlantic Canada History
Titles in Print: 18
Total Employees: 2 (plus summer intern)
Internship Contact: Phillip Buckner, Editor
Internships Offered: Salaried
Yearly Number Available: 1 (depending on grant money)
Departments: Editorial
Duties/Responsibilities: Intern will learn to edit proofs, assist in mailings, distribute and ship books and work on a word processor.
Application Procedure: Call contact for more information.

ACROPOLIS BOOKS LTD.
Colortone Building
2400 17th Street NW
Washington, DC 20009
202-387-6805

Types of Publishing: Nonfiction
Titles in Print: 300
Total Employees: 65
Internship Contact: John Hackl, President
Internships Offered: Salaried

Yearly Number Available: 1
Applications Received: 10-15
Period of Availability: Summer
Duration: 7-8 weeks
Qualifications: College juniors or seniors.
Application Procedure: Send cover letter/resume to contact.

ADDISON-WESLEY PUBLISHING COMPANY, INC.
Route 128
Reading, MA 01867
617-944-3700

The Minority Internship Program offers professional level summer internships to qualified minority students.

Types of Publishing: College Text, School, Professional, Reference, Scholarly, Scientific/Technical, Software, Trade (hardcover and paperbound)
Titles in Print: 6,500
Total Employees: 1,300
Internship Contact: Jeffrey Kline, Sr. Human Resource Representative
Internships Offered: Salaried
Yearly Number Available: 6
Departments: Editorial, Marketing, Sales, Production (and others)
Period of Availability: Summer
Duration: Summer
Duties/Responsibilities: There are a variety of challenging and educational positions available in the departments listed above. These opportunities offer the student a wide range of publishing experiences to enhance their understanding of the industry. There are positions available in the Reading, MA office as well as the office outside San Francisco.
Qualifications: College sophomore or junior with an interest in publishing— top quality students who are looking for positive summer jobs.
Application Procedure: Send cover letter and resume to contact.
Application Deadline: April 1.
Decision Date: May 1.

ALLYN & BACON INC.
A subsidiary of Simon & Schuster
7 Wells Avenue
Newton, MA 02159
617-455-1200

Titles in Print: 300
Total Employees: 300

Internship Contact: Stacey Liebertal, Human Resource Specialist
Internships Offered: Salaried
Yearly Number Available: 2-3
Departments: Production, Permissions
Applications Received: 10-15
Period of Availability: Summer
Duration: 6-8 weeks
Duties/Responsibilities: Permissions—phone work. Production—layout on Macintosh computer, coordinate pieces of book.
Qualifications: College sophomores—seniors.
Application Procedure: Send cover letter/resume to contact.

AMACOM BOOK DIVISION
The American Management Association
135 West 50th Street
New York, NY 10020
212-903-8018

Types of Publishing: Trade nonfiction—Management and Business
Titles in Print: 300
Total Employees: 700+
Internship Contact: George Harmon, Director of Human Resource Development
Internships Offered: Non-Salaried (Stipend)
Yearly Number Available: 15 each quarter
Internship Departments: Varied, from Editorial to Marketing
Applications Received: 40-60
Duration: 12 weeks
Duties/Responsibilities: Communication skills important. In all departments, interns receive meaningful project assignments. Depending on the department, interns may attend seminars.
Qualifications: College juniors, seniors and graduate students.
Application Procedure: Send cover letter/resume to contact.

ASHLEY BOOKS, INC.
30 Main Street
Port Washington, NY 11060
516-883-2221

Types of Publishing: College Text, El/Hi, Professional, Religious, Scholarly, Scientific/Technical, Trade (hardcover and paperback), Health Field fiction & nonfiction
Titles in Print: 390

Total Employees: 200
Internship Contact: Joan Calder, Vice President
Internships Offered: Non-Salaried
Yearly Number Available: 2
Departments: Editorial, Public Relations, Clerical
Applications Received: 75
Period of Availability: Flexible
Duties/Responsibilities: Editorial—Proofing, copy editing, editing. Public Relations—Booking authors, arranging print interviews. Clerical—Variety of office projects.
Qualifications: College students (all years acceptable).
Application Procedure: Send cover letter/resume to contact.

ROBERT BENTLEY, INC.
1000 Massachusetts Avenue
Cambridge, MA 02138
617-547-4170

Types of Publishing: College Text, Professional, Reference, Scientific/Technical
Titles in Print: 135
Total Employees: 11
Internship Contact: D. Waite, Personnel Manager
Internships Offered: Both
Yearly Number Available: 1
Applications Received: 10-15
Period of Availability: Summer
Duration: 6-8 weeks
Qualifications: College juniors, seniors and graduates.
Application Procedure: Send cover letter/resume to contact.

BERKLEY PUBLISHING GROUP
See listing for Putnam Berkley Group

BRANDEN PUBLISHING COMPANY
17 Station Street—Box 843
Brookline Village, MA 02147
617-734-2045

Types of Publishing: College Text, Professional, Reference, Religious, Scholarly, Scientific/Technical, Software, Trade (hardcover and paperback)
Titles in Print: 260
Total Employees: 8

Internship Contact: Adolph Caso, President

Internships Offered: Non-Salaried

Yearly Number Available: 2

Departments: All

Applications Received: 3-4

Period of Availability: Year-round

Duties/Responsibilities: As this is a very small company, interns must do everything the publisher does, from imputing data to editing, book design and shipping.

Qualifications: College juniors, seniors and graduates.

Application Procedure: Send cover letter/resume to contact.

Application Deadline: Ongoing

CAMBRIDGE UNIVERSITY PRESS
40 West 20th Street
New York, NY 10011
212-924-3900

Types of Publishing: Children's, College, Professional, Reference, Religious, Scholarly, Scientific/Technical, Software, Journals

Titles in Print: 9,000

Total Employees: 834

Internship Contact: George Andreou, Internship Coordinator

Internships Offered: Non-Salaried (students can arrange for college credit)

Yearly Number Available: 2

Departments: Editorial, Production, Marketing

Applications Received: 12-15

Period of Availability: Summer

Duration: 8 weeks

Duties/Responsibilities: Interns rotate through all departments and every effort is made to give them "hands-on" experience. Clerical duties are part of the work in all departments. Students receive letter of evaluation at end of program.

Qualifications: College freshmen—juniors. Must type 40 wpm.

Application Procedure: Send cover letter/resume to contact.

Application Deadline: March

Decision Date: May

THE CAREER PRESS INC.
62 Beverly Road—P.O. Box 34
Hawthorne, NJ 07507
201-427-0229

Types of Publishing: Reference, Educational, Business & Financial How-To (paperback)

Titles in Print: 50

Internship Contact: Carol Eagleson

Internships Offered: Both

Yearly Number Available: 1-2

Internship Departments: All

Applications Received: 25

Period of Availability: Year-round

Duration: 8-10 weeks

Duties/Responsibilities: Interns get involved in a variety of projects, from inputting data to helping edit, publicize and sell books. Definitely "hands-on" experience requiring intelligence, communication and interpersonal skills and a love of publishing and books.

Qualifications: College juniors and seniors; returnees to the work force; career changers. Must type (at least 40-50 wpm) and be computer literate. Famil-iarity with Macintosh computer and Microsoft Word a definite plus.

Application Procedure: Send cover letter/resume and samples of writing to contact. No phone calls please.

Application Deadline: Two-three months before intern would like to start. By April 15 for summer.

MARCEL DEKKER, INC.
270 Madison Avenue
New York, NY 10016
212-696-9000

Types of Publishing: College Text, El/Hi, Professional, Reference, Scholarly, Scientific/Technical, Software, Trade (hardcover & paperback)

Titles in Print: 2,215

Total Employees: 372

Internship Contact: Maureen Smith, Personnel Recruiter

Internships Offered: Non-Salaried

Yearly Number Available: 2

Departments: All

Applications Received: 10

Period of Availability: School year only

Duration: September-June

Duties/Responsibilities: Interns do general office work and float from department to department as needed. In this way, they receive a solid overview of the publishing field.

Qualifications: High school students only. Knowledge of general office work and typing skills helpful.

Application Procedure: Call contact.

Application Deadline: Calls usually made in Sept.

Decision Date: Until January

DIAL BOOKS FOR YOUNG READERS
A division of E.P. Dutton
2 Park Avenue
New York, NY 10016
212-397-8000

Types of Publishing: General Trade, Fiction and Nonfiction (hardcover & paperback)

Titles in Print: 500

Total Employees: 600

Internship Contact: Shelly Sadler, Personnel Department

Internships Offered: Salaried

Yearly Number Available: 1

Applications Received: 50

Period of Availability: Summer

Duration: 3 months

Duties/Responsibilities: 50% secretarial; light editing; reading/evaluating manuscripts; working on editorial bulletin.

Qualifications: College juniors and seniors.

Application Procedure: Send cover letter/resume to contact.

Decision Date: May 1

E.P. DUTTON
See listing for Penguin USA

F & W PUBLICATIONS INC.
1507 Dana Avenue
Cincinnati, OH 45207
513-531-2222

Types of Publishing: Books—art and writing titles and directories; book clubs; magazines; home study courses.

Titles in Print: 300

Total Employees: 175
Internship Contact: Kathy Schneider, Personnel Director
Internships Offered: Salaried ($200/wk)
Yearly Number Available: 7-8
Departments: Advertising, Art, Book Club Promotion, Magazine and Book Editorial, Circulation
Applications Received: 100
Period of Availability: Summer
Duties/Responsibilities: Non-artists: Copy editing, proofreading, writing promotion copy, analysis, research, correspondence, clerical. Interns in Art Department do paste-up, layout and simple design projects. All interns attend planning and analysis meetings. Some assistance is offered to locate housing.
Qualifications: Students must have completed their junior year, be enrolled in good standing in a Business, English (or other liberal arts program) or Journalism program. Seniors planning to attend graduate school may also apply.
Application Procedure: Send cover letter, resume and writing samples to contact.
Application Deadline: January 31
Decision Date: March 1

FABER & FABER, INC.
50 Cross Street
Winchester, MA 01890
617-721-1427

Types of Publishing: Trade
Titles in Print: 800
Total Employees: 8
Internship Contact: Susan Nash, VP
Internships Offered: Non-Salaried
Period Of Availability: Year-round
Application Procedure: Send cover letter/resume to contact.

FARRAR, STRAUS & GIROUX, INC.
19 Union Square West
New York, NY 10003
212-741-6900

Types of Publishing: Children's, Trade (hardcover & paperback)
Titles in Print: 300+
Total Employees: 100
Internship Contact: Peggy Miller, Office Manager

Internships Offered: Non-Salaried

Yearly Number Available: 1-10

Departments: All

Period of Availability: Year-round

Duration: Flexible

Duties/Responsibilities: Can range from clerical to reading manuscripts. No writing involved. Interns provide general help wherever needed.

Qualifications: High school graduates.

Application Procedure: Call Ms. Miller, then send cover letter and resume.

Application Deadline: No formal deadline.

GALE RESEARCH CO.
Book Tower
Detroit, MI 48226
313-961-2242

Types of Publishing: Indexes, encyclopedias, directories.

Titles in Print: 5,000

Total Employees: 700

Internship Contact: Ms. Nancy Turnblom

Internships Offered: Salaried (Students must arrange for college credit with their school.)

Yearly Number Available: 25

Departments: Editorial, Research

Period of Availability: Year-round

Duration: One semester (quarter); prefer full-time.

Duties/Responsibilities: Interns act as assistants in the Editorial and Research departments. (Some computer interns have recently been accepted.) The co-op program involves clerical duties associated with publishing, proofreading and some writing.

Qualifications: Prefer liberal arts majors. Typing of 35 wpm required. High school and/or college yearbook experience is helpful but not required. Good eye for detail a plus. Proof of co-op experience helpful—students must arrange for credit with their co-op or career placement office.

Application Procedure: Send cover letter, resume, transcript and writing samples. Writing samples must be analytical (book reviews, critiques of someone else's writing, etc.) 5-10 pages long and not journalism or creative writing samples. They must be complete (i.e., no excerpts).

Application Deadline: 1-2 months prior to when intern wants to start.

Decision Date: Approx. 2 weeks before start of semester.

GREENWOOD PRESS
88 Post Road—Box 5007
Westport, CT 06881
203-226-3571

Types of Publishing: Professional, Academic

Titles in Print: 10,000+

Total Employees: 102

Internship Contact: Carole Bronson, VP Production

Internships Offered: Salaried

Yearly Number Available: 1-2

Applications Received: 10-15

Period of Availability: Summer

Duration: 10-12 weeks

Qualifications: College sophomores—seniors, usually recommended by local college co-op programs.

Application Procedure: Send cover letter/resume to contact.

Application Deadline: Usually filled rapidly, so the earlier the better.

GUERNICA EDITIONS
P.O. Box 633, Station N.D.G.
Montreal, PQ H4A 3R1
514-256-5599

Types of Publishing: Children's, College Text, Mass Market Paperback, Reference, Scholarly, Trade (hardcover & paperback)

Titles in Print: 80

Total Employees: 3

Internships Offered: Salaried (Stipend)

Yearly Number Available: 1-2

Departments: Editorial

Period of Availability: Year-round

Duration: 12 weeks

Duties/Responsibilities: Mostly clerical, some proofreading, no writing.

Qualifications: College students (sophomores—seniors); literature major preferred.

Application Procedure: Cover letter/resume to contact.

Application Deadline: Flexible

RICHARD D. IRWIN, INC.
1818 Ridge Road
Homewood, IL 60430
312-798-6000

Types of Publishing: College Text, Professional, Trade (hardcover)
Titles in Print: 1,500
Total Employees: 400
Internship Contact: Personnel Dept.
Internships Offered: Both
Yearly Number Available: 10
Departments: Editorial, Business, Graphic Design (assignment geared to major—Art, English, Business, etc.)
Applications Received: 60-100
Period of Availability: Summer
Duration: 4-6 weeks, sometimes longer.
Duties/Responsibilities: Each department head works directly with the intern and assigns various duties and responsibilities.
Qualifications: Varies by department, but college students (sophomores—seniors) preferred; freshmen not usually considered.
Application Procedure: Call Personnel. Cover letters and resumes accepted. Referrals from in-house department heads considered. Interviews conducted at various universities.
Application Deadline: Late April.

LITTLE, BROWN AND COMPANY
A subsidiary of Time Inc.
34 Beacon Street
Boston, MA 02106
617-227-0730

Types of Publishing: Children's, Professional, Reference, Trade (hardcover)
Total Employees: 645
Internship Contact: Rebecca Parker, Employment Manager
Internships Offered: Salaried
Yearly Number Available: 5-10
Departments: All (Sales, Promotion, Editorial, etc.)
Applications Received: 20-30
Period of Availability: Summer; month of January
Duration: 12 weeks (summer)
Duties/Responsibilities: Interns in any department must perform clerical duties, perhaps even act as "go-fers." Interns are considered for full-time positions after graduation.

Qualifications: College students with genuine interest in publishing. Must type 40-50 wpm. Experience on high school or college yearbook or newspaper helpful.

Application Procedure: Send cover letter/resume to contact—no typos!

Application Deadline: End of March.

Decision Date: First week of April.

MAXWELL-MACMILLAN PUBLISHING COMPANY
866 Third Avenue
New York, NY 10022
212-702-2000

Types of Publishing: Children's, College Text, El/Hi, Mass Market Paperback, Professional, Reference, Religious, Scholarly, Software, Scientific/Technical, Trade (hardcover & paperback), Music Books

Titles in Print: 2,600+

Total Employees: 2,300

Internship Contact: Abby Miller, Personnel Manager

Internships Offered: Non-Salaried

Yearly Number Available: 5-7

Departments: All

Applications Received: 10-20

Period of Availability: Summer

Duration: 6-8 weeks

Qualifications: Minorities only.

Application Procedure: Send cover letter/resume plus transcript (if possible) to contact.

MASTERY EDUCATION
85 Main Street
Watertown, MA 02172
617-926-0329

Types of Publishing: Elementary

Titles in Print: 500

Total Employees: 63

Internship Contact: Elena Wright, Managing Editor

Internships Offered: Non-Salaried (Stipend)

Yearly Number Available: 2

Applications Received: 10-20

Period of Availability: Year-round

Duration: 16 weeks

Duties/Responsibilities: We work closely with students in their particular area of expertise. If they are interested in Production, for example, they will work with paste-ups, layouts, etc. In editorial, they will work with specs, proof-reading, etc. If qualified, some students are given the opportunity to write short articles for print.

Qualifications: College sophomores—seniors. Strong English background for Editorial interns; demonstrable art skills for Graphics interns.

Application Procedure: Send cover letter/resume to contact. Include writing samples if applying for Editorial internship.

Application Deadline: Flexible according to student's schedule.

MERRILL PUBLISHING COMPANY
A subsidiary of Bell & Howell Company
936 Eastwind Avenue
Westerville, OH 43081
614-890-1111

Types of Publishing: College Text, El/Hi

Titles in Print: 4,000+

Total Employees: 650

Internship Contact: James Green, Senior Administrator

Comments: Internship program not formed yet, but ideas are being considered. Call contact and state your interest.

WILLIAM MORROW & COMPANY, INC.
105 Madison Avenue
New York, NY 10016
212-889-3050

Types of Publishing: Children's, Nonfiction, Travel, Fiction, Adult Trade

Titles in Print: 2,500

Total Employees: 170

Internship Contact: Mrs. Barbara E. Spence, Personnel Director

Internships Offered: Both (Summer $100/wk; school-year for college credit only)

Yearly Number Available: 5

Departments: All

Applications Received: 50-75

Period of Availability: Year-round

Duration: Summer—May-August. Fall or Winter—one semester or Winter or Spring Break.

Duties/Responsibilities: Summer internships: Interns are provided with an in-depth work experience in several departments of the company. A weekly schedule is set up giving each intern the opportunity to work in most of the

Morrow departments and divisions for a minimum of 2-4 weeks each. In Editorial, the work will include the reading of unsolicited manuscripts, writing reader's reports, typing and sending out formal rejection letters to authors.

The work itself varies from department to department, but includes typing, filing, operating a copy machine and answering phones. Other internships: Most of the above also applies, except interns usually work in one department only. Students must receive college credit for internship and are responsible for their own living arrangements.

Qualifications: College students, any year, with some office experience during summers or after school. Typing 35-40 wpm minimum.

Application Procedure: Resume and cover letter stating interest, background and a confirmation from their college that they will receive credits for the internship to Ms. Spence. Candidates interviewed during mid-Winter Break.

Application Deadline: January 15.

THE C.V. MOSBY COMPANY
11830 Westline Industrial Drive
St. Louis, MO 63108
314-872-8370

Types of Publishing: College Text, Professional, Reference, Scientific/Technical, Software

Titles in Print: 2,000

Total Employees: 650

Internship Contact: Lucy Morgan, Employment Supervisor

Internships Offered: Non-Salaried

Yearly Number Available: 4

Departments: All

Applications Received: 12

Period of Availability: Year-round

Duration: One semester

Duties/Responsibilities: Interns really have a chance to get involved. They will generally work on a special project which would vary from department to department—such as writing, putting together product kits, gathering financial information, etc.

Qualifications: College seniors preferred.

Application Procedure: Send cover letter/resume to contact.

Application Deadline: Flexible.

THOMAS NELSON PUBLISHERS
Elm Hill Pike at Nelson Place
Nashville, TN 37214
615-889-9000

Types of Publishing: Audio/Visual, Children's, Mass Market Paperback, Paperback Trade, Reference, Religious

Total Employees: 235

Internship Contact: Susan Andrews, Personnel Administrator

Internships Offered: Commission Sales

Yearly Number Available: 500

Applications Received: 2,000-2,500

Period of Availability: Summer

Duration: Summer (2-3 months)

Duties/Responsibilities: After traveling to Nashville for training, interns travel to their assigned territory. They purchase their stock of books wholesale and sell retail, getting hands-on sales and marketing experience. While they are trained in the basics of sales and marketing and given detailed product information, they are essentially on their own once they reach their territory and may attempt a number of creative sales strategies. Obviously, total compensation is based on actual sales.

Qualifications: College students, any year.

Application Procedure: Interviews are conducted on campuses nationwide. Check with your career office to see when (or if) an interview is scheduled for your campus, or call company to locate nearby campus.

Application Deadline: Mid- to late-April.

Decision Date: Interns accepted until the last two weeks of school (May-June).

OXFORD UNIVERSITY PRESS
200 Madison Avenue
New York, NY 10016
212-679-7300

Types of Publishing: College Text, Professional, Reference, Scholarly, Trade (hardcover & paperback), ESL

Total Employees: 280

Internship Contact: Nancy O'Connor, Personnel Director

Period of Availability: Summer

Application Procedure: Call contact for more information.

POCKET BOOKS
A division of Simon & Schuster
1230 Avenue of the Americas
New York, NY 10022
212-698-7000

Types of Publishing: Consumer Group, Production, Trade

Titles in Print: 100,000+

Total Employees: 600

Internship Contact: Mr. Cary Gregory, Recruiter

Internships Offered: Salaried ($100/wk)

Yearly Number Available: 40

Departments: All—Art, Editorial, Business, Marketing & Sales

Applications Received: 200+

Period of Availability: Summer

Duration: 8 weeks

Duties/Responsibilities: This company tries to make sure their internships are a real learning experience for the student. A wide range of potential positions are available in New York and New Jersey. Managers attempt to give interns hands-on experience. Some routine duties are required.

Qualifications: College students—no seniors. Some graduate students accepted. Typing usually required. Strong general, academic and extracurricular background necessary, as there is very stiff competition for these openings. Program is not geared to those returning to the work force or career changers.

Application Procedure: Application must be submitted to contact. Write for it or check with your college career office to see if they have applications on hand. Students are asked to choose three areas of interest and we make our best effort to place them in one of those fields.

Application Deadline: April 1

Decision Date: May 31

PRENTICE-HALL, INC.
See listing for Simon & Schuster, Inc.

PRICE/STERN/SLOAN PUBLISHERS, INC.
360 North LaCienega Blvd.
Los Angeles, CA 90048
213-657-6100

Types of Publishing: Children's, Trade, Cookbooks, Automotive, Photography, Nonfiction, Juvenile, Educational, Gift & Novelties, Audio/Video, Electronic, Interactive, Calenders

Titles in Print: 1,500

Total Employees: 300
Internship Contact: Spencer Humphrey, Director of Business Affairs
Internships Offered: Non-Salaried
Yearly Number Available: 5-6
Period of Availability: Year-round
Duration: 10 weeks
Qualifications: College students.
Application Procedure: Send cover letter/resume to contact.
Application Deadline: None.

THE PUTNAM BERKELEY GROUP
200 Madison Avenue
New York, NY 10016
212-951-8400

Types of Publishing: Children's, Trade (hardcover and paperback), General Fiction and Nonfiction
Total Employees: 500
Internship Contact: Grace Heelan, Production Manager
Internships Offered: Non-Salaried ($500 lunch stipend)
Yearly Number Available: 6
Departments: Editorial, Publicity, Production, Managing Editor's Office, Children's
Applications Received: 50-100
Period of Availability: Summer
Duration: 12 weeks
Duties/Responsibilities: Interns spend three weeks in four departments (Editorial, Publicity, Production, Managing Editor's Office). One intern is specifically assigned to the Children's department.
Qualifications: College students (generally juniors returning to school for their senior year).
Application Procedure: Send cover letter/resume to contact. An interview is required.
Application Deadline: April 1
Decision Date: Mid-May

RODALE PRESS, INC.
33 East Minor Street
Emmaus, PA 18098
215-967-5171

Types of Publishing: Gardening, Health, Fitness, Sports

Titles in Print: 900
Total Employees: 1,070
Internship Contact: Paul Ivankevich, Manager of Personnel Services
Internships Offered: Salaried
Yearly Number Available: 15-20
Departments: Research, Writing, Business Analysis, Promotion, Public Relations, Production, Art
Period of Availability: Summer (Year-round applicants considered)
Duration: 10 weeks (approx. June 4—August 10)
Duties/Responsibilities: Interns will be directly involved in a number of areas of publishing, not just doing clerical tasks.
Qualifications: College juniors. Journalism major helpful. Students with marketing background may qualify for positions in Creative area. Business interns should have relevant degree or course background.
Application Procedure: Editorial—Send cover letter, resume and three magazine-style writing samples (preferably published campus or community work). Art—Send cover letter and resume (must have a portfolio available).
Application Deadline: Mid-April for summer programs..

SCHOLASTIC, INC.
730 Broadway
New York, NY 10003
212-505-3000

Types of Publishing: Educational
Total Employees: 1,300 nationwide (500 in NY)
Internship Contact: Julius James, Recruiter
Internships Offered: Non-Salaried
Yearly Number Available: 1
Departments: All
Applications Received: 25
Period of Availability: Summer (10-12 weeks)
Application Procedure: Send cover letter/resume to contact.

SIMON & SCHUSTER, INC.
1230 Avenue of the Americas
New York, NY 10022
212-698-7000

Types of Publishing: Audio/Visual, Children's, College, El/Hi, Mass Market Paperback, Professional, Reference, Scientific/Technical, Trade (hardcover & paperback)
Titles in Print: 8,000+

Total Employees: 9,000

Internship Contact: Barbara Learner, Manager of Corporate Communications

Internships Offered: Salaried ($100/wk).

Yearly Number Available: 40-50

Departments: Editorial, Sales, Marketing, Business, Art & Design, Production, Publicity

Applications Received: 80-100

Period of Availability: Summer

Duration: 8 weeks

Duties/Responsibilities: Attend meetings, complete various assignments and research according to department. Some interns get actual projects to work on. Informal educational seminars.

Qualifications: College freshmen—seniors.

Application Procedure: Company application must be used. Contact Human Resources department and refer to Program's name (see above).

Application Deadline: April 1

Decision Date: May 31

STEMMER HOUSE PUBLISHERS, INC.
2627 Caves Road
Owings Mills, MD 21117
301-363-3690

Types of Publishing: Audio/Cassettes, Children's, Trade (hardcover & paperback)

Titles in Print: 156

Total Employees: 4

Internship Contact: Barbara Holdridge, President

Internships Offered: Both

Yearly Number Available: 1-2

Departments: Editorial

Applications Received: 10

Period of Availability: Flexible

Duration: 10 weeks

Qualifications: College juniors or seniors. No returnees to the work force or career changers

Application Procedure: Send cover letter/resume to contact.

Application Deadline: Flexible.

JEREMY P. TARCHER, INC.
9110 Sunset Blvd.—Suite 250
Los Angeles, CA 90069
213-273-3274

Types of Publishing: Trade (hardcover & paperback)
Total Employees: 20
Internship Contact: Pat Bryer, Controller & Personnel Director
Internships Offered: Non-Salaried
Yearly Number Available: 1
Applications Received: 12-14
Period of Availability: Year-round
Duration: 8 weeks
Qualifications: College sophomores—seniors.
Application Procedure: Send cover letter/resume to contact.
Application Deadline: Flexible.

TRANSACTION PUBLISHERS
Rutgers University
New Brunswick, NJ 08903
201-932-2280

Types of Publishing: Professional, Reference, Scholarly, Social Scientific/Technical
Titles in Print: 2,000
Total Employees: 24
Internship Contact: Scott Bromson, Sr. Vice President
Internships Offered: Salaried
Yearly Number Available: 1
Applications Received: 4-6
Period of Availability: Summer
Duration: 6-10 weeks
Qualifications: College sophomores—seniors.
Application Procedure: Send cover letter/resume to contact.
Application Deadline: Beginning of Spring semester.

UNIVERSITY OF NEW MEXICO PRESS
Journalism Building
Albuquerque, NM 87131
505 277-2346

Types of Publishing: Professional, Scholarly

Titles in Print: 375
Total Employees: 20
Internship Contact: David V. Holtby, Associate Director
Internships Offered: Non-Salaried
Yearly Number Available: 1-2
Applications Received: 10-14
Period of Availability: Summer
Duration: 8-12 weeks
Application Procedure: Send cover letter/resume to contact.
Application Deadline: Flexible.

THE UNIVERSITY OF NORTH CAROLINA PRESS
Box 2288
Chapel Hill, NC 27515-2288
919-966-3561

Types of Publishing: University Press
Titles in Print: 450
Total Employees: 30
Internship Contact: Matthew Hodgson, Director
Internships Offered: Non-Salaried
Yearly Number Available: 1-2
Applications Received: 10-14
Period of Availability: Summer
Duration: 8-10 weeks
Qualifications: College sophomores—seniors.
Application Procedure: Send cover letter/resume to contact.
Application Deadline: Flexible.

UNIVERSITY PRESS OF AMERICA, INC.
4720 Boston Way
Lanham, MD 20706
301-459-3366

Types of Publishing: College, Professional, Library, Trade Lines
Titles in Print: 3,000
Total Employees: 50
Internship Contact: James E. Lyons, Publisher
Internships Offered: Non-Salaried
Yearly Number Available: 1
Applications Received: 25-30

Period of Availability: Summer
Duration: 7-10 weeks
Application Procedure: Send cover letter/resume to contact.
Application Deadline: Flexible.

VIKING PENGUIN INC.
40 West 23rd Street
New York, NY 10010
212-337-5200

Types of Publishing: Trade
Titles in Print: 5,000
Total Employees: 168
Internship Contact: Joyce Smith, Personnel
Internships Offered: Non-Salaried (Commutation expenses reimbursed)
Yearly Number Available: 1-2
Departments: Adult Editorial, Children's, Design, Managing Editor Depts.
Period of Availability: Summer
Duration: 12 weeks
Duties/Responsibilities: Intern will assist with clerical work in department. May read and evaluate manuscripts in editorial or participate in projects appropriate to other departments. A strong effort is made for intern to participate in meetings and have the opportunity to interact with experienced staff in departments they are assigned to.
Qualifications: College freshmen—seniors. Interest in book publishing; typing and office skills.
Application Procedure: Send cover letter/resume to contact.
Application Deadline: April
Decision Date: May

WARREN, GORHAM & LAMONT, INC.
One Penn Plaza
New York, NY 10119
212-971-5177

Types of Publishing: Professional; periodicals and magazines in the fields of accounting, banking and financial, law, real estate, etc.
Titles in Print: 250
Total Employees: 600
Internship Contact: Anna Pugliese, Employment Specialist
Internships Offered: Salaried ($225-$250/wk)
Yearly Number Available: 10-12 (NY, Boston)

Departments: Marketing, Human Resources, Finance, Editorial

Applications Received: 50

Period of Availability: Summer

Duties/Responsibilities: Entry-level opportunities will provide introduction to functional area, as well as exposure to the publishing industry. Many positions require some administrative skills, such as typing (40 wpm).

Qualifications: Bright, energetic, good communication skills. Prior office experience helpful, but not necessary.

Application Procedure: Send cover letter/resume to contact; indicate area of interest. Qualified candidates will be contacted and asked to visit the company for an interview.

Application Deadline: February 1.

JOHN WILEY & SONS, INC.
605 Third Avenue
New York, NY 10158
212-850-6000

Types of Publishing: Professional, College, Trade (paperback), Software, Technical, Scientific, Business, Encyclopedias

Titles in Print: 10,000

Internship Contact: Susan Fisher, Sr. Employ. Rep.

Internships Offered: Salaried ($225/wk)

Yearly Number Available: 5-10

Departments: All

Applications Received: 50-60

Period of Availability: Summer

Duration: 10 weeks

Duties/Responsibilities: Internships are project- oriented and involve various duties, some of them clerical, depending on each department. Company hopes interns return after graduation as full-time employees.

Qualifications: College students (undergraduates only).

Application Procedure: Send cover letter/resume to contact. Interview required; typing and spelling test given at time of interview.

Application Deadline: April 1

Decision Date: May

WILLIAMS & WILKINS
428 East Preston Street
Baltimore, MD 21202
301-528-4212

Types of Publishing: Medical, Allied Health, Nursing

Titles in Print: 750+

Total Employees: 78

Internship Contact: Paul Shiah, Human Resources Dept.

Internships Offered: Both (Summer internships are paid; those during school year are for credit only.)

Yearly Number Available: 5-10

Departments: All

Period of Availability: Year-round

Duration: 3 months (summer); 1 semester (school year)

Duties/Responsibilities: Vary widely according to student's ability. Basically interns are there to "lighten the load" for regular employees, especially during summers due to vacation schedules, and to help out wherever needed—primarily clerical duties.

Qualifications: High school or college students with good common sense. Clerical and/or personal computer skills very helpful.

Application Procedure: Send cover letter/resume to contact.

Application Deadline: Late April.

SPECIAL NOTE: RANDOM HOUSE DOES INDEED HAVE AN INTERNSHIP PROGRAM, THOUGH IT IS STATED EARLIER THAT IT DOES NOT. PLEASE CONTACT GREG GIANGRANDE AT 212-572-2610 FOR FURTHER DETAILS, WHICH ARRIVED TOO LATE FOR INCLUSION IN THIS VOLUME.

Section 4

Appendices
And Index

12

U.S & Canadian
Trade Organizations

**THE ADVERTISING CLUB
OF NEW YORK**
155 East 55th Street—Suite 202
New York, NY 10022
212-935-8080

**ADVERTISING RESEARCH
FOUNDATION**
3 East 54th Street—15th Floor
New York, NY 10022
212-751-5656

**ADVERTISING WOMEN
OF NEW YORK**
153 East 57th Street
New York, NY 10022
212-593-1950

**AGRICULTURAL PUBLISHERS
ASSOC.**
111 East Wacker Drive
Chicago, IL 60601
312-644-6610

**ALBERTA PUBLISHERS
ASSOCIATION**
#123, 10523 100 Avenue
Edmonton, AB T5J 0A8
403-424-5060

**ALBERTA WEEKLY NEWS-
PAPERS ASSOC.**
#380, 4445 Calgary Trail S.
Edmonton, AB T6H 5R7
403-434-8746

**AMERICAN ADVERTISING
FEDERATION**
1400 K Street—Suite 1000
Washington, DC 20005
202-898-0089

**AMERICAN ASSOC. OF AD-
VERTISING AGENCIES** (4A's)
666 Third Avenue
New York, NY 10017
212-682-2500

**AMERICAN ASSOCIATION OF
SUNDAY AND FEATURE
EDITORS**
c/o Jack Rickman
The Houston Chronicle
801 Texas Avenue
Houston, TX 77002
713-220-7601

**AMERICAN BOOKSELLERS
ASSOCIATION**
137 West 25th Street
New York, NY 10001
212-463-8450

**AMERICAN INSTITUTE
OF GRAPHIC ARTS**
1059 Third Avenue—3rd Floor
New York, NY 10021
212-752-0813

**AMERICAN JEWISH PRESS
ASSOCIATION**
c/o No. Cal. Jewish Bulletin
88 First Street—3rd Floor
San Francisco, CA 94105
415-957-9340

**AMERICAN NEWSPAPER
PUBLISHERS ASSOC.
And ANPA FOUNDATION**
Dulles Airport—Box 17407
Washington, DC 20041
703-648-1000

**AMERICAN NEWS-
WOMEN'S CLUB**
1607 22nd Street NW
Washington, DC 20008
202-332-6770

AMERICAN PRESS INSTITUTE
11690 Sunrise Valley Drive
Reston, VA 22091
703-620-3611

**AMERICAN SOCIETY OF
JOURNALISTS AND AUTHORS**
1501 Broadway—Suite 1907
New York, NY 10036
212-997-0947

**AMERICAN SOCIETY OF
MAGAZINE EDITORS**
575 Lexington Avenue
5th Floor
New York, NY 10022
212-752-0055

**AMERICAN SOCIETY
OF MAGAZINE
PHOTOGRAPHERS**
419 Park Avenue South
New York, NY 10016
212-889-9144

**AMERICAN SOCIETY OF
NEWSPAPER EDITORS**
Dulles Airport
P.O. Box 17004
Washington, DC 20041
703-648-1145

**AMERICAN SOCIETY OF
PICTURE PROFESSIONALS**
Grand Central Station
Box 5283
New York, NY 10063
212-685-3870

ART DIRECTORS CLUB
250 Park Avenue South
New York, NY 10003
212-674-0500

**ASSOCIATED PRESS
MANAGING EDITORS**
50 Rockefeller Plaza
New York, NY 10020
212-621-1552

**ASSOCIATED PRESS
SPORTS EDITORS**
P.O. Box 1129
Auburn, AL 36831
205-844-4607

**ASSOCIATION OF AMERICAN
EDITORIAL CARTOONISTS**
c/o Ed Stein, Rocky Mountain News
400 West Colfax
Denver, CO 80204
303-892-5000

**ASSOCIATION OF AMER-
ICAN PUBLISHERS**
220 East 23rd Street, 2nd Floor
New York, NY 10010
212-689-8920

**ASSOCIATION OF AMERICAN
UNIVERSITY PRESSES**
584 Broadway—Suite 410
New York, NY 10012
212-941-6610

**ASSOCIATION OF BOOK
PUBLISHERS OF BRITISH
COLUMBIA**
1622 West 7th Avenue
Vancouver, BC V6J 1S5
604-734-1611

**ASSOCIATION OF BUSINESS
PUBLISHERS**
Attn: Phyllis L. Reed, Manager,
Placement & Education Services
675 Third Avenue—Suite 400
New York, NY 10017
212-661-6360

**ASSOCIATION OF CANADIAN
EDITORIAL CARTOONISTS**
81 Metcalfe Street,
9th Floor
Ottawa, ON K1P 6K7

**ASSOCIATION OF CANADIAN
PUBLISHERS**
260 King Street East, 2nd Floor
Toronto, ON M5A 1K3
416-361-1408

**ASSOCIATION OF JEWISH
BOOK PUBLISHERS**
c/o Union of American Hebrew
Congregations
838 Fifth Avenue
New York, NY 10021
212-249-0100

**ASSOCIATION OF MANITOBA
BOOK PUBLISHERS**
100 Arthur Street, #204
Winnipeg, MB R3B 1B3
204-947-3335

**ASSOCIATION OF
NEWSPAPER CLASSIFIED
ADVERTISING MANAGERS**
Box 267
Danville, IL 61834-0267
217-442-2057

**ASSOCIATION OF PUBLI-
CATION PRODUCTION
MANAGERS**
Grand Central Station, Box 5016
New York, NY 10017

**ASSOCIATION OF THE
GRAPHIC ARTS**
5 Penn Plaza—20th Floor
New York, NY 10001
212-279-2100

**ASSOCIATION FOR PROMO-
TION OF INDEPENDENT
PRINTING & PUBLISHING**
27 Queen Street East, #702
Toronto, ON M5C 2M6

ATLANTIC COMMUNITY NEWSPAPERS ASSOCIATION
#614, 5161 George Street
Halifax, NS B3J 1M7
902-422-3122

ATLANTIC PUBLISHERS ASSOCIATION
1741 Barrington Street, 4th Floor
Halifax, NS B3J 2A4
902-420-0711

BLACK WOMEN IN PUBLISHING
P.O. Box 6275
FDR Station, NY 10150
212-772-5951

BOOK & PERIODICAL DEVELOPMENT COUNCIL
34 Ross Street, #200
Toronto, ON M5T 1Z9
416-595-9967

THE BOOK ARTS SOCIETY OF CANADA
571 Jarvis Street
Toronto, ON M4Y 2J1

BOOK PUBLISHERS' PROFESSIONAL ASSOCIATION
78 Sullivan Street
Toronto, ON M5T 1C1

THE BOOKMAKERS OF TORONTO
47 Manor Road West
Toronto, ON M5P 1E6
416-485-9225

BRITISH COLUMBIA & YUKON COMMUNITY NEWSPAPERS ASSOC.
#812, 207 West Hastings St.
Vancouver, BC V6B 1H7
604-669-9222

THE BUSINESS PRESS EDUCATIONAL FOUNDATION
675 Third Avenue—Suite 400
New York, NY 10017-5704
212-682-4410

BUSINESS/PROFESSIONAL ADVERTISING ASSOCIATION
100 Metroplex Drive
Edison, NJ 08817
201-985-4441

THE CANADIAN ASSOCIATION OF PHOTOGRAPHERS & ILLUSTRATORS IN COMMUNICATIONS
400 Eastern Avenue, #250
Toronto, ON M4M 1B9
416-462-3677

CANADIAN BOOKBINDERS & BOOK ARTISTS GUILD
P.O. Box 1142, Stn. F
Toronto, ON M4Y 2T8
416-885-9508

CANADIAN BOOK INFORMATION CENTRE
260 King Street East, 3rd Floor
Toronto, ON M5A 1K3
416-362-6555

CANADIAN BOOK INFORMATION CENTRE (EAST)
1741 Barrington Street
4th Floor
Halifax, NS B3J 2A4
902-420-0688

CANADIAN BOOK INFORMATION CENTRE (PRAIRIES)
#205, 100 Arthur Street
Winnipeg, MB R3B 1B3
204-943-3767

**CANADIAN BOOK INFOR-
MATION CENTRE (WEST)**
1622 West 7th Avenue
Vancouver, BC V6J 1S5
604-734-2011

**CANADIAN BOOK
PUBLISHERS' COUNCIL**
45 Charles Street East, 7th Floor
Toronto, ON M4Y 1S2
416-964-7231

**CANADIAN BOOK SELLERS
ASSOCIATION**
301 Donlands Avenue
Toronto, ON M4J 3R8
416-467-7883

CANADIAN BUSINESS PRESS
100 University Avenue, #508
Toronto, ON M5J 1V6
416-593-5497

**CANADIAN COMMUNITY
NEWSPAPERS ASSOC.**
88 University Avenue, #705
Toronto, ON M5J 1T6
416-598-4277

**CANADIAN DAILY NEWSPA-
PER PUBLISHERS ASSOC.**
890 Yonge Street, #1100
Toronto, ON M4W 3P4
416-923-3567

**CANADIAN PRINTING
INDUSTRIES ASSOC.**
75 Albert Street, #906
Ottawa, ON K1P 5E7
613-236-7208

CARTOONISTS GUILD
The Graphic Artists Guild
11 West 20th Street—8th Floor
New York, NY 10011
212-463-7730

CHICAGO BOOK CLINIC
100 East Ohio Street
Chicago, IL 60611
312-951-8254

CHILDREN'S BOOK COUNCIL
P.O. Box 706
New York, NY 10276
212-254-2666

**CHRISTIAN BOOKSELLERS
ASSOCIATION**
2620 Venetucci Blvd., P.O. Box 200
Colorado Springs, CO 80901
719-576-7880

**CHRISTIAN BOOKSELLERS
ASSOCIATION (CANADA)**
1574 Lincoln Road
Windsor, ON N8Y 2J4
519-254-8692

COSMEP
P.O. Box 703
San Francisco, CA 94101
415-922-9490

**EDITORIALFREELANCERS
ASSOCIATION INC.**
Madison Square Station, Box 2050
New York, NY 10159
212-677-3357

**ENGLISH LANGUAGE
PUBLISHERS ASSOC.**
c/o McGill-Queen's University Press
855 Sherbrooke Street West
Montreal, PQ H3A 2T7
514-393-3750

**GAY AND LESBIAN
PRESS ASSOCIATION**
P.O. Box 8185
Universal City, CA 91608
818-902-1476

GRAPHIC ARTISTS GUILD
11 West 20th Street—8th Floor
New York, NY 10011
212-463-7730

**INTERNATIONAL ASSOCI-
ATION OF FRENCH-
LANGUAGE UNIVERSITY
PRESSES**
Universite de Montreal
Boite Postale 6128
Montreal, PQ H3C 3J7
514-343-6111

**INTERNATIONAL CIRCU-
LATION MANAGERS
ASSOCIATION**
Dulles Airport
P.O. Box 17420
Washington, DC 20041
703-648-1150

**INT'L NEWSPAPER ADVER-
TISING & MARKETING
EXECUTIVES**
Dulles Airport
P.O. Box 17210
Washington, DC 20041
703-648-1178

**INTERNATIONAL NEWS-
PAPER FINANCIAL
EXECUTIVES**
Dulles Airport
P.O. Box 17573
Washington, DC 20041
703-648-1159

**INTERNATIONAL NEWS-
PAPER MARKETING
ASSOCIATION**
Dulles Airport
P.O. Box 17422
Washington, DC 20041
703-648-1094

**INTERNATIONAL SOCIETY
OF WEEKLY NEWSPAPER
EDITORS**
Department of Journalism
Northern Illinois University
DeKalb, IL 60115
815-753-1925

**INVESTIGATIVE REPORTERS
AND EDITORS**
School of Journalism
100 Neff Hall
University of Missouri
Columbia, MO 65211
314-882-2042

LITERARY PRESS GROUP
260 King Street East
Toronto, ON M5A 1K3
416-361-1408

MAGAZINES CANADA
777 Bay Street—7th Floor
Toronto, ON M5W 1A7
416-596-2641

**MAGAZINE PUBLISHERS
ASSOCIATION**
575 Lexington Avenue
New York, NY 10022
212-752-0055

**MANITOBA COMMUNITY
NEWSPAPERS ASSOC.**
#204, 254 Edmonton Street
Winnipeg, MB R3C 3Y4
204-947-1691

**NATIONAL ASSOCIATION
OF AD. PUBLISHERS**
111 East Wacker Drive
Suite 600
Chicago, IL 60601
312-644-6610

NATIONAL ASSOCIATION OF
BLACK JOURNALISTS/
NATIONAL ASSOCIATION OF
HISPANIC JOURNALISTS
c/o Knight Ridder, Inc.
One Hearst Plaza
Miami, FL 33101
305-376-3934

NATIONAL ASSOCIATION OF
PUBLISHERS REPRE-
SENTATIVES
P.O. Box 1692
Grand Central Station
New York, NY 10163
212-944-9685

NATIONAL CONFERENCE OF
EDITORIAL WRITERS
6223 Executive Boulevard
Rockville, MD 20852
301-984-3015

NATIONAL FEDERATION
OF PRESS WOMEN
Box 99
Blue Springs, MO 64015
816-229-1666

NATIONAL NEWSPAPER
ASSOCIATION
1627 K Street NW
Washington, DC 20006
202-466-7200

NATIONAL PRESS CLUB
National Press Building
529 14th Street NW
Washington, DC 20045
202-662-7500

NATIONAL PRESS
PHOTOGRAPHERS ASSOC.
Box 1146
Durham, NC 27702
919-489-3700

NATIONAL SPORTSCASTERS
AND SPORTWRITERS ASSOC.
Box 559
Salisbury, NC 28144
704-633-4275

NEWSPAPER ADVERTISING
BUREAU
1180 Avenue of the Americas
New York, NY 10036
212-921-5080

NEWSPAPER ADVERTISING
EXECUTIVES ASSOC. OF
CANADA
890 Yonge Street, #1100
Toronto, ON M4W 3P4
416-923-3567

NEWSPAPER ADVERTISING
SALES ASSOCIATION
c/o Cresmer, Woodward, O'Mara &
Ormsbee
750 Third Avenue
New York, NY 10017
212-949-6400

NEWSPAPER ASSOCIATION
MANAGERS
Dulles Airport
P.O. Box 17407
Washington, DC 20041
703-648-1123

NEWSPAPER MARKETING
BUREAU, INC.
21 King Street East, #2100
Toronto, ON M5C 1A2
416-364-3744

NEWSPAPER PERSONNEL
RELATIONS ASSOCIATION
Dulles Airport
P.O. Box 17407
Washington, DC 20041
703-648-1069

**NEWSPAPER RESEARCH
COUNCIL**
601 Locust—Suite 1000
Des Moines, IA 50309
515-245-3828

**NEW YORK RIGHTS AND
PERMISSIONS GROUP**
c/o Gale Research Company
Penobscot Building
Detroit, MI 48226
313-961-2242 X6813
(Jeanne Gough, Prod. Mgr.)

THE ONE CLUB
3 West 18th Street—3rd Floor
New York, NY 10011
212-255-7070

**ONTARIO (& QUEBEC)
COMMUNITY NEWSPAPERS
ASSOCIATION**
P.O. Box 451
Oakville, ON L6J 5A8
416-844-0184

ONTARIO PRESS COUNCIL
36 King Street East—4th Floor
Toronto, ON M5C 2L9
416-665-6551

**ONTARIO PUBLISHERS
EDUCATIONAL
REPRESENTATIVES
ASSOCIATION**
c/o Maureen Huntington
P.O. Box 671
Don Mills, ON M3C 2T6

**ONTARIO REPORTERS'
ASSOCIATION**
P.O. Box 353
Simcoe, ON N3Y 4L2
416-385-3456

**PUBLIC RELATIONS SOCIETY
OF AMERICA**
33 Irving Place
New York, NY 10003
212-995-2230

PUBLISHERS AD CLUB
c/o Cathy Grunewald
St. Martin's Press
175 Fifth Avenue
New York, NY 10010
212-674-5151

**PUBLISHERS PUBLICITY
ASSOCIATION INC.**
c/o Susan Richman
MacMillan Publishing Co.
866 Third Avenue
New York, NY 10022
212-702-6757

**PUBLISHERS PUBLICITY
CLUB**
c/o Arlynn Greenbaum
Little, Brown & Company
205 Lexington Avenue
New York, NY 10016
212-683-0660

**SALES AND MARKETING
EXECUTIVES INT'L**
446 Statler Office Tower
Cleveland, OH 44115
216-771-6650

**SASKATCHEWAN WEEKLY
NEWSPAPERS ASSOCIATION**
P.O. Box 1000
Humboldt, SK S0K 2A0
306-682-3408

**THE SOCIETY OF AMERICAN
GRAPHIC ARTISTS**
32 Union Square—Room 1214
New York, NY 10003
516-725-3990

SOCIETY OF GRAPHIC DESIGNERS
P.O. Box 2245, Stn. D
Ottawa, ON K1P 5W4
613-238-4997

THE SOCIETY OF ILLUSTRATORS
128 East 63rd Street
New York, NY 10021
212-838-2560

THE SOCIETY OF NATIONAL ASSOCIATION PUBLICATIONS
3299 K Street NW—7th Floor
Washington, DC 20007
202-965-7510

THE SOCIETY OF NEWSPAPER DESIGN
Dulles Airport
P.O. Box 17290
Washington, DC 20041
703-648-1308

THE SOCIETY OF PROFESSIONAL JOURNALISTS
53 West Jackson Blvd.
Suite 731
Chicago, IL 60604
312-922-7424

THE SOCIETY OF PUBLICATION DESIGNERS
60 East 42nd Street—Suite 1416
New York, NY 10165
212-983-8585

SOCIETY FOR SCHOLARLY PUBLISHING
1918 18th Street NW—Suite 21
Washington, DC 20009
202-328-3555

SUCCESSFUL MAGAZINE PUBLISHER'S GROUP
P.O. Box 2029
Tuscaloosa, AL 35403
205-349-2990

WHITE HOUSE CORRESPONDENTS ASSOCIATION
National Press Building
529 14th Street NW
Room 1067
Washington, DC 20045
202-737-2934

WHITE HOUSE NEWS PHOTOGRAPHERS ASSOCIATION
Ben Franklin Station
P.O. Box 7119
Washington, DC 20044
202-634-7940

WOMEN IN COMMUNI- CATIONS, INC.
2101 Wilson Boulevard
Suite 417
Arlington, VA 22201
703-528-4200

WOMEN IN SCHOLARLY PUBLISHING
c/o American Assoc. of University Presses
Stanford, CA 94305
415-723-9434

WOMEN'S NATIONAL BOOK ASSOCIATION, INC.
160 Fifth Avenue
New York, NY 10010
212-675-7804

13

U.S. & Canadian
Trade Publications

ACTUALITE CANADA
#400, 55 Bloor Street West
Toronto, ON M4W 1A5
416-923-4000

ADVERTISING AGE
Crain Communications, Inc.
740 North Rush Street
Chicago, IL 60611
312-649-5200

ADWEEK
A/S/M Communications
49 East 21st Street—11th Floor
New York, NY 10010
212-529-5500

AMERICAN BOOKSELLER
Booksellers Publishing, Inc.
137 West 25th Street
New York, NY 10001
212-463-8450

AMERICAN PRINTER
MacLean Hunter Pub. Co.
29 North Wacker Drive
Chicago, IL 60606
312-726-2802

APPLIED ARTS
20 Holly Street, #208
Toronto, ON M4S 3B1
416-488-1163

ART DIRECTION
10 East 39th Street—6th Floor
New York, NY 10016
212-889-6500

ART PRODUCT NEWS
In-Art Publishing Company
P.O. Box 117
St. Petersburg, FL 33731
813-821-6064

BOOKLIST
American Library Assoc.
50 East Huron Street
Chicago, IL 60611
312-944-6780

BOOKSTORE JOURNAL
(Official publication of the Christian
Booksellers Assoc.)
CBA Service Group, Inc.
2620 Venetucci Blvd., P.O. Box 200
Colorado Springs, CO 80901
719-576-7880

BUSINESS MARKETING
Crain Communications, Inc.
220 East 42nd Street
New York, NY 10017
212-210-0100

**CANADIAN AUTHOR
& BOOKMAN**
Canadian Authors Assoc.
121 Avenue Road, #104
Toronto, ON M5R 2G3
416-926-8084

**CANADIAN LIBRARY
JOURNAL**
Canadian Library Assoc.
200 Elgin Street
Ottawa, ON K2P 1L5
613-232-9625

**CANADIAN PRINTER
AND PUBLISHER**
777 Bay Street
Toronto, ON M5W 1A7
416-596-5884

**CANADIAN PUBLISHERS'
DIRECTORY**
#213, 56 The Esplanade
Toronto, ON M5E 1A7
416-364-3333

**COLUMBIA JOURNALISM
REVIEW**
Columbia University
School of Journalism
Room 700
New York, NY 10027
212-854-7216

CONTENT
33 Charkay Street
Nepean, ON K2E 5N4
613-727-6907

CREATIVE
Magazines/Creative, Inc.
37 West 39th Street
Suite 604
New York, NY 10018
212-840-0160

THE EDITORIAL EYE
Editorial Experts, Inc.
66 Canal Center Plaza
Suite 200
Alexandria, VA 22314
703-683-0683

EDITOR & PUBLISHER
11 West 19th Street
New York, NY 10011
212-675-4380

EDUCATIONAL MARKETER
Knowledge Industry Publications, Inc.
701 Westchester Avenue
White Plains, NY 10604
914-328-9157

**ELECTRONIC COMPOSITION
& IMAGING**
200 Yorkland Blvd.
Willowdale, ON M2J 1R5
416-492-5777

EMERGENCY LIBRARIAN
P.O. Box 46258, Stn. G
Vancouver, BC V6R 4G6
604-734-0255

**EP&P: THE MAGAZINE FOR
ELECTRONIC PUBLISHING**
MacLean Hunter Publishing Corp
300 West Adams
Chicago, IL 60606
312-726-2802

**FOLIO: THE MAGAZINE FOR
MAGAZINE MANAGEMENT**
Folio Magazine Pub. Corp.
6 River Bend—P.O. Box 4949
Stamford, CT 06907-0949
203-358-9900

G MAGAZINE
C.P. 1122, Place Bonaventure
Montreal, PQ H5A 1G4
514-397-0537

GRAPHIC ARTS MONTHLY
Technical Publishing
249 West 17th Street
New York, NY 10011
212-645-0067

GRAPHIC DESIGN: USA
Kaye Publishing Corporation
120 East 56th Street—Suite 440
New York, NY 10022
212-759-8813

THE GRAPHIC MONTHLY
#205, 2065 Dundas Street East
Mississauga, ON L4X 2W1
416-625-7070

GRAPHIS
Published in Zurich, Switzerland, but
sold in most well-stocked art supply
stores. Covers the best art and design
work internationally.

INSIDE MEDIA
Hanson Publishing Group
6 River Bend—P.O. Box 4949
Stamford, CT 06907-0949
203-358-9900

**LIBRARY JOURNAL /
SCHOOL LIBRARY JOURNAL**
R.R. Bowker Company
249 West 17th Street
New York, NY 10011
212-645-9700

**LOCUS: THE NEWSPAPER OF
THE SCIENCE FICTION FIELD**
Locus Publications, Inc.
Box 13305
Oakland, CA 94661
415-339-9196

**MAGAZINE AND
BOOKSELLER**
North American Pub. Co.
322 Eighth Avenue
New York, NY 10001
212-620-7330

**MAGAZINE DESIGN
AND PRODUCTION**
Globecom Publishing, Ltd.
8340 Mission Road—Suite 106
Prarie Village, KS 66206
913-642-6611

LE MAITRE IMPRIMEUR
480 Mont Royal Avenue East
Montreal, PQ H2J 1W4
514-842-2751

**MARKETING AND
MEDIA DECISIONS**
Act III Publishers
401 Park Avenue South, 7th Floor
New York, NY 10016
212-545-5100

MARKETING NEWS
American Marketing Assoc.
250 South Wacker Drive, Suite 200
Chicago, IL 60606
312-648-0536 (Association)
312-993-9517 (Editorial)

MASTHEAD
2065 Dundas Street East, #205
Mississauga, ON L4X 2W1
416-625-7070

**MIN: MEDIA INDUSTRY
NEWSLETTER**
MIN Publishing Inc.
145 East 49th Street—Suite 7B
New York, NY 10017
212-751-2670

NEWS CANADA
#400, 55 Bloor Street West
Toronto, ON M4W 1A5
416-923-4000

NEWS PHOTOGRAPHER
Nat'l Press Photographers Assoc.
1446 Conneaut Avenue
Bowling Green, OH 43402
419-372-0308

NICHES
Independent Publishers League
Drawer 5007
Bend, OR 97708

PHOTO DESIGN
Billboard Publications
1515 Broadway
New York, NY 10036
212-764-7300

PRESS REVIEW
P.O. Box 368, Stn. A
Toronto, ON M5W 1C2
416-368-0512

PRESSTIME
Amer. Newspaper Pub. Assoc.
11600 Sunrise Valley Drive
Reston, VA 22091
703-648-1074

PRINTACTION
200 Yorkland Blvd.
Willowdale, ON M2J 1R5
416-492-5777

PRINT & HOW
R.C. Publications, Inc.
104 Fifth Avenue—9th Floor
New York, NY 10011
212-463-0600

PRINTING IMPRESSIONS
North American Pub. Co.
401 North Broad Street
Philadelphia, PA 19108
215-238-5300

PRINTING PRODUCT GUIDE
777 Bay Street
Toronto, ON M5W 1A7
416-596-5884

PUBLICATION PROFILES
777 Bay Street
Toronto, ON M5W 1A7
416-596-5890

**PUBLIC RELATIONS
JOURNAL**
33 Irving Place
New York, NY 10003
212-995-2230

THE PUBLISHER
#705, 88 University Avenue
Toronto, ON M5J 1T6
416-598-4277

PUBLISHERS AUXILIARY
National Newspaper Assoc.
1627 K Street, #400
Washington, DC 20006
202-466-7200

PUBLISHERS WEEKLY
R.R. Bowker Company
249 West 17th Street
New York, NY 10011
212-645-9700

PUBLISHING TRADE
Coast Publishing Inc.
1680 SW Bayshore Blvd.
Port St. Lucy, FL 34984
407-879-6666

THE QUILL
Society of Professional Journalists
53 West Jackson Blvd.
Suite 731
Chicago, IL 60604
312-922-7751

QUILL & QUIRE
#213, 56 The Esplanade
Toronto, ON M5E 1A7
416-364-3333

QUILL & SCROLL
(International Honorary Society for
High School Journalists)
School of Journalism and Mass
Communications
University of Iowa
Iowa City, IA 52242
319-335-5795

RESOURCE MAGAZINE
18 Van Dusen Blvd.
Toronto, ON M8Z 3E5
416-231-7796

SCHOLARLY PUBLISHING
University of Toronto Press
5201 Dufferin Street
Downsview, ON M3H 5T8
416-667-7781

SELLING SPACE
JB & Me
P.O. Box 3879
Manhattan Beach, CA 90266
213-546-1255

**SMALL PRESS: THE
MAGAZINE OF INDEPENDENT
IN-HOUSE DESKTOP
PUBLISHING**
Meckler Publishing Corporation
11 Ferry Lane West
Westport, CT 06880
203-226-6967

SOURCES
9 St. Nicholas Street, #402
Toronto, ON M4Y 1W5
416-964-7799

**STANDARD RATE & DATA
(SRDS)**
Standard Rate & Data Service, Inc.
3004 Glenview Road
Wilmette, IL 60091
312-256-6067

STEP-BY-STEP GRAPHICS
Dynamic Graphics, Inc.
6000 North Forest Park Drive
Peoria, IL 616144
309-688-2300

**THE ST. LOUIS JOURNALISM
REVIEW**
8380 Olive Boulevard
St. Louis, MO 63132
314-991-1699

STUDIO MAGAZINE
124 Galaxy Blvd.
Toronto, ON M9W 4Y6
416-675-1999

TARGET MARKETING
North American Pub. Co.
401 North Broad Street
Philadelphia, PA 19108
215-238-5300

**UPPER AND LOWER CASE
(U&lc)**
International Typeface Corp.
2 Dag Hammarskjold Plaza—3rd
Floor
New York, NY 10017
212-371-0699

**WASHINGTON JOURNALISM
REVIEW**
2233 Wisconsin Avenue NW, #442
Washington, DC 20007
202-333-6800

THE WRITER
120 Boylston Street
Boston, MA 02116
617-423-3157

WRITERS DIGEST
F & W Publications
1507 Dana Avenue
Cincinnati, OH 45207
513-531-2222

14

Index To Articles And Listings

The Career Press

America's Premiere Publisher of books on:

- Career & Job Search Advice
- Education
- Business "How-To"
- Financial "How-To"
- Study Skills
- Careers in Advertising, Book Publishing, Magazines, Newspapers, Marketing & Sales, Public Relations, Business & Finance, the Travel Industry and much, much more.
- Internships

If you liked this book, please write and tell us!

And if you'd like a copy of our FREE catalog of nearly 100 of the best career books available, please call us (Toll-Free) or write!

THE CAREER PRESS
62 BEVERLY RD.,
PO BOX 34
HAWTHORNE, NJ 07507
(Toll-Free) 1-800-CAREER-1 (U. S. only)
201-427-0229
FAX: 201-427-2037